W9-AQN-114

The Integrated Life

The mind of man is framed even like the breath
And harmony of music. There is a dark
Invisible workmanship that reconciles
Discordant elements, and makes them move
In one society.

WORDSWORTH, The Prelude, I, 351-55

THE INTEGRATED LIFE

Essays, Sketches, and Poems
by Thomas Percival Beyer

Essay Index Reprint Series

 BOOKS FOR LIBRARIES PRESS
FREEPORT, NEW YORK

STANDARD BOOK NUMBER:
8369-1393-0

LIBRARY OF CONGRESS CATALOG CARD NUMBER:
75-93317

PRINTED IN THE UNITED STATES OF AMERICA

FOR

the Hamline friends
who have been my students and teachers
since 1906
in S11, U31, and U4

Foreword

THOMAS P. BEYER'S students remember him best for stimulating them in two directions — toward worthwhile reading and toward creative writing. Or maybe it is better said that travel toward both is in the same direction. Dr. Beyer stressed creative *reading*, too. In one of the stimulating essays in this book he says: "Creative reading is the soul of the writer plus the soul of the reader."

At Hamline Dr. Beyer and reading have been almost synonymous. He proposed the general reading course in 1921 and directed it for twelve years. Students alert to this form of inspiration found exciting delight not only in the reading outside their regular courses but in the discussions with faculty members which followed. Colleagues and off-campus friends also came under the provocative influence of Dr. Beyer, and his guidance has been freely and frequently acknowledged. The breadth of his own reading is one of the amazing phenomena of this restless age. The general reading course idea now has been revived and a bulletin on reading has been prepared by a committee of which Dr. Beyer was chairman. Two discriminating lists are contained therein: "Voices of the Living Past" and "Voices of the Present." Dr. Beyer's course of recent years, "Catching Up With the Classics," has evoked heartening response from sophomores and upperclassmen.

In creative writing the results of his helpfulness are more easily traced. They appeared for many years in student entries for the Bridgman prizes. Dr. Beyer has edited four volumes of poems which earned awards in that competition and all have won wide, favorable comment from critics.

Last spring in an *Atlantic Monthly* poetry contest open to all colleges, Hamline students took two of the first four places. Margaret Snyder, a Hamline graduate whose splendid story of a pioneer Minnesota town, *The Chosen Valley*, has just been published, inscribed her book: "For Thomas P. Beyer, who set me the long task of understanding."

When Dr. Beyer was honored in 1947 for his long, fruitful association with Hamline University, a fund was gathered for publication of Hamline-connected writings. It was unanimously agreed that a collection of Dr. Beyer's own essays, poems, and speeches should be the first venture, and here it is. No attempt has been made to bring them up to date. They appear as they were written, some of them nearly a generation ago — full of the flavor and wisdom of a truly honorable teacher and friend.

It should not be supposed, however, that Dr. Beyer's contributions to Hamline have been confined to reading and writing. Soon after his connection with the English department in 1906 he helped coach field and track teams. Later he was tennis coach for many years. He was chairman of the college committee on athletics from 1908 to 1920 and helped to establish the Tri-State Conference (Minnesota and the two Dakotas) and then the Minnesota Conference. From 1915 to 1934 he was editor of the *Hamline University Bulletin*, a quarterly, and personally handled the catalogue number during that time, with the exception of two years of leave. In 1918-19 he was an administrator of the National War Labor Board and in 1924-25 he served as an exchange professor at Tsing Hua College, Peking. He had a prominent part in founding a number of Hamline organizations, among them the Faculty Club, English Club, Quill Club, Literary Board, and Kappa Phi. In every literary promotion, including the successive magazines, he had a leading part.

In most of his Hamline connections he has not stood alone but as one of a talented family. Mrs. Beyer, who was

Flora Winifred Lynn of Tarkio, Missouri, before their marriage in 1908, has been his inspiration these many years. Two sons, Lynn and Carlyle, could hardly escape profiting from their home influence. Both graduated from Hamline and both went to Oxford as Rhodes scholars. Both served with distinction in the armed services during the recent war. All these Beyers have honored Hamline. All have avoided the condition which Dr. Beyer denounces in this book: the closed compartment mind.

By these poor words let some confession be made of the debt to the *pater familias* owed by student, colleague, and friend. I have been all three.

GEORGE L. PETERSON

Minneapolis
November 15, 1948

Table of Contents

The Integrated Life

The Integrated Life

ON ONE thing, and one thing only, nearly all articulate men and women at the middle of this fourth decade of the twentieth century are agreed. The life of man is amorphous, "without form and void." Tennyson thought man

An infant crying in the night
An infant crying for the light
And with no language but a cry.

But today the realist poet finds him an animal with no language but a grunt, or it would be more exact to the realist poet to say a machine with no language but a very bad squeak. The hearth is swept clean, the sanctuary is empty, the future is hopeless unless this or that or the other is done and done quickly. We merely say, "The king is dead"; we do not add, "Long live the king," for we do not want a new king.

We do not agree on the particular king that is dead. Each one proves that such and such kings are dead — Jehovah or Darwin or Democracy or Mussolini or Lenin or Franklin Roosevelt or Reason or Intuition or Monism or Pragmatism or Humanism or Modernism. There is no Aaron's Rod turned serpent to eat up the other serpents; they eat up each other. We are like enthusiastic beginners in chess, so intent on attack that we do not think of defense, and in the end the board is clear. We suddenly realize that there is no king left on the board; that contrary to the rules of the game he has not simply been checkmated, he has disappeared. To be sure this situation is impossible in good

NOTE. Based on the Cap and Gown Day Address at Hamline University, April 1935.

3

chess. But *impossible* is a theoretical word, and practical but bewildered players recognize nothing but that the kings are gone.

The players now divide roughly into two groups: first, those who are glad because they do not believe in government of any sort, and desire only, amoeba-like, to expand and contract at pleasure. They seem not to know, or to know but dimly that the amoeba too is bound by rules. Second, those who passionately desire a king. Some of them charge that the rules of the game *must* have been broken, because it is impossible for both sides to lose. And yet since 1919 many have learned that that anomalous result *can* and *has* come about; we have yet to comprehend that war, and more especially a peace like Versailles — which passed all understanding — must always show a loss to both and all sides. Others more pragmatically admit that the kings *are* dead, but they insist that we must set up a new stable government if we are to exist at all as personalities.

II

WHAT MUST I DO TO BE SAVED? This is still the all-important question for a man and a nation. It is childish to cavil at the theological savor of "saved." A great deal of modern fiction describes people who have no touch with traditional religion, who avow, or would avow if their creator would ever give them enough intelligence to put together the haziest thought, that there is no life other than the present good life of the senses. They are thoroughly mechanistic, thoroughly scientific, thoroughly modern. They cannot conceive of anything better than good food, good wine, soft flesh, and social or economic power. But what they all passionately crave and agonize over through hundreds of pages is the extension of their youth for the full enjoyment of all these pleasures for the maximum number of years. In the language of the ignored Scripture, they want more life, and

4

they want it more abundantly. They are as desirous of being saved as the Puritan or the new humanist, and they are as zealously though always blindly in search of atonement, at-one-ment. It is a human need and constant crying demánd to hold and consolidate and preserve what we have.

Those who have developed a spiritual life put a higher estimate on what they have, and consequently on what they desire. Being more conscious of abstract intellectual processes, more skillful in their operation, and more hopeful of their results, they think and talk more of at-one-ment, but they are no more obsessed by its necessity than are the novelistic characters of such a book as Louis Bromfield's *24 Hours* (first published as *Shattered Glass*). *24 Hours* is by no means the worst example that might be adduced by a new humanist, for it is written by a genuine artist. But it is one long headache of sex and frustration. Not one of the characters knows what it is all about, but every one yearns to enjoy the flesh as long as science and a generous unearned income can preserve their bodies against ultimate and complete decay.

III

Teachers, particularly teachers of English composition, have a peculiar relation to this serious malady of modern life. Unity, Coherence, and Emphasis are the shibboleths that rhetoricians since Aristotle have harped upon. They are no more important because Aristotle announced them than poetry is important because Homer composed it, or than the Canon of Difference is scientifically valuable because John Stuart Mill phrased it. They are *there*. They describe the way words or paints or stone or sounds behave when an artist takes them in hand.

Teachers of English composition are sometimes blamed a little sharply for ranging over creation and pretending to teach everything, for imitating Carlyle's Teufelsdrockh, who was "Professor der Allerleiwissenschaft." The timider souls in the profession draw back and disclaim any such ambitious intention. They shiver, Oh dear no, we do not pretend to *know* anything about psychology or physics or history or economics or philosophy or ethics; we merely try to get our students to *think*. Think what? Oh, just think!

There are too many of these limber minds in the profession, intellectual mollycoddles with no clear knowledge outside the texts and pure literature, with no convictions and no passions.

But there are other teachers who are willing to accept the garland of satire and bind it on their brows. However presumptuous they may seem to others, they know that they do not pretend to a knowledge of *everything*; but they also know that when they glorify and magnify Unity, Coherence, and Emphasis they are aiming to teach *all things*. Not every thing, but *all things*. Composition, startling as it may sound to many of its professors, has nothing to do with spelling, grammar, or punctuation, or the tricks of plot building, or the magazine market. It means in the writer's art exactly what it means in every art, the placing together of elements with unity, coherence, and emphasis in such manner as to form a whole. Teachers of this type agree with the first group that their job is to teach students to think; but unlike the limber liberals, they believe that when one thinks, he must think *something*. Furthermore they are not content with seeing a student in the agony of thinking; they must try to furnish him with the necessary tools and materials for effective thinking. They may be patently and egregiously wrong; they often are. But unless they passionately aim to be right and to help guide right, they belong with all the other "blind mouths, who scarce themselves know how to hold a sheep-hook." Good composition on paper is unthinkable without good composition in thought, and good composition in thought requires that the composing mind have unity, coherence, and emphasis. So it will be seen that there is close similarity, indeed a virtual identity, between the ability to compose thoughts on paper and the ability to compose the life of the composer.

IV

More than a quarter of a century in college should teach one something. When one considers that four years is the term of "an education" for the student, whose shortcomings have been so widely flaunted, he may expect either the four-year student's wisdom multiplied sixfold in the twenty-five-year teacher, or his ignorance increased in the same proportion.

To express a truth is not the same as to learn that truth. During my academic life there has never been a time, unless it was in the war years, when the chapel rostrum did not resound to denunciations of the closed-compartment mind. Presidents, professors, itinerant lecturers, all hold to the theory that religion, for instance, must leaven the whole life of the student. Ministers have for a long time quoted approvingly, "He prayeth best who loveth best," but their applications almost invariably showed until recently that what they really meant was, "He loveth best who prayeth best." To translate religion into conduct is the theme of an aria of the highest respectability; but if a student or teacher in an American college holds that modern society is fundamentally unethical, and particularly unchristian, that is, if he really believes it as Tolstoi and Walter Rauschenbusch and Upton Sinclair believed it, and has the courage to act upon his belief, he is a local pariah — and very soon he ceases to be local. Milton's immortal panegyric to freedom of speech in *Areopagitica* is popular word music, but is not understood by one percent of those who sing it.

Three illustrations of this failure to integrate may be briefly recited:

7

1. Education is continually spoken of as threefold: physical, intellectual, and spiritual; or sometimes fourfold: physical, intellectual, moral, and spiritual.

> *Let us not alway say,*
> *Spite of the flesh today,*
> *I strove, made head, gained ground upon*
> * the whole.*
> *As the bird wings and sings,*
> *We cry, "All good things*
> *Are ours; nor soul helps flesh more now*
> *Than flesh helps soul."*

These lines from Browning's "Rabbi Ben Ezra" decorate many a discourse whose author apparently harbors the opinion that there is in it more poetry than truth.

2. Closely associated with the above logical failure, as mutual cause and effect, is the evil of specialization.

The conspicuous absence from college faculties of the old-fashioned scholar is generally rationalized by an invocation of the vast gains in every field of knowledge during the last hundred years. It is manifestly impossible, it is said, that a single individual in this age of rapid progress should know well more than one thing. A popular cliché announces that the average high school youth knows more about physics than Sir Isaac Newton.* Every modern shoemaker must stick to his last; or rather, there is no modern shoemaker; there is instead only a factory of specialists who know individually how to cut a sole or stitch a certain seam. When a tyro in history like H. G. Wells or Lewis Mumford tries to comprehend the whole life of man, he is treated to a fine display of supercilious scorn by professionals; and even

---

*I must not here pause to examine the logical implications of such statements. Obviously one of them is that the schoolboy of the next generation will know more than Einstein, and so on *ad infinitum.* Whereas it must be clear to all but the most superficial mind that the schoolboy, like Newton and Einstein, knows only what he comprehends, and no more.

when a more learned Whitehead or Jeans steps out of his field, the eyebrows are lifted, though with somewhat more decorum.

Seventy-five years ago Matthew Arnold preached some fine sermons, not all of which have been discredited. One of them was this: He who knows nothing but the Bible does not know the Bible. This text suggests a general truth that is never directly controverted. The mechanism of the human eye recognizes its validity, for if it would see a faint light clearly, or see it at all, it must focus a little to one side. "Something about everything and everything about something" is another cliché that pays lip-homage to the truth, but the sad fact remains that our college faculties are made up of uneducated and partially (an enlightening ambiguity) educated specialists. A trained scientist may have the immature religious ideas of his childhood, an instructor in the social studies may be devoid of any understanding of what constitutes intellectual honesty in composition, and an English teacher may think he can teach how to think without having any thoughts of his own that the student can take interest in.

3. A phenomenon closely related to specialization is the lack of integration in the curriculum. Related "departments" ignore each other in planning "courses"; and, even more ridiculous, different "courses" in the same "department" overlap and repeat content material, while at the same time great gaps yawn unstopped because the budget does not permit securing the proper specialist. Many experiments are under way here and there to remedy this particular evil, but scrutiny of college catalogues shows that it is endemic.

This is enough to suggest what I mean when I say that the closed-compartment mind is as typical of college organization as it is of the woof of modern life, upon which it aims to set a pattern.

9

V

One of the surest symptoms of mental disorderliness (if not actually mental disorder) is constant resort to vague and muzzy phrases. Nothing is more certain than that a thought clearly conceived must be capable of clear expression. Minds as variously constituted as those of Montaigne, Pascal, Thoreau, Poe, Samuel Butler, and Croce knew and vigorously maintained this truth: that clear thinking results in clear writing. In composition classes this is generally a red rag. Some student is sure he has thoughts which he cannot express. In the last few years I have had less trouble than formerly in convincing him that what he has is not a thought, but a vague and inchoate feeling which his meager vocabulary prevents from taking on the angular outline of a thought. A vague phrase means something that is not fully and completely a thought. In the realm of art there is a place for such phrases, but not for the purposes of exposition. One of the worst offenders is "the higher things of life." I listened a short while ago to America's most popular preacher in an address directed to a large group of the leisure class wintering in the South. It contained everything: Greece, Rome, Carthage, Cleopatra, Saint Augustine, the Pilgrim Fathers, George Washington, the spread of the American empire, the League of Nations, wartime bellicosity and peacetime pacifism, with preparedness — and of course the heaviest shot was a tribute to the soul of American business. The peak phrase was this masterpiece: "We need untainted money, *kissed by the chemistry of the higher things.*" This is always sure-fire. "The higher things" remove the taint from any money.

When the announced business of a college is "to perfect the scholar," one might be led to expect clarified diction, words as things. The business is to think, and thinking can be expressed only in words as "hard as cannon-balls." But "the higher things of life" resound more mellifluously from the college rostrum, if possible, than from the pulpit or the lecture platform. And the terribly disconcerting observation to anyone who is really in earnest about the value of "perfecting the scholar" is that those who invoke "the higher things" generally imply that they are quite unrelated to the main business for which the student is in college, that they will be found only when his eyes are closed and his intelligence on holiday. The classroom may drone that "the Word is not the Thing," but the inspired voice of prophecy erases that lesson by frequent illustrations that words are the "higher things."

Nature has a habit of integrating day and night, sunshine and rain, summer and winter. Man's first attempts at specialization in life were not unnatural, or unrelated to natural sequence. Fasts and feasts, work and play, love-making and continence, all have a normal composition, exemplifying unity, coherence, and emphasis under primitive conditions. The religious rites of the savage were specialized and seasonal, but his convictions were constant. He did not secularize six sevenths of his life. He had special memorial days, but he did not forget to reverence constantly the virtues to which he occasionally paid special homage. So far as I know, he had no Mother's Day or Father's Day, but in a matriarchal society the mothers ruled every day, and in a patriarchy the Old Man was boss. He did not invent the Apple Week, but he knew enough to eat fruit when he could get it. He did not have a Go to Church Week or a Day of Prayer for Colleges. He invoked his gods specially every day he needed their help to send rain or to confuse his enemy, but the devotion to his religion and the business of educating his young went on steadily.

The most practical and American of all men, Benjamin Franklin, laid down thirteen virtues, which he practiced in turn for a week at a time, but he went over the whole gamut four times a year, and his ultimate purpose was coherence, the welding of all, industry, frugality, temperance, and so on, into the character of an ideal personality. He succeeded to the extent of his vision. Jesus, the carpenter of Nazareth, had a loftier conception of the ideal man, a conception which he closely realized by keeping the thought of God and his brother ever in mind and attending synagogue very rarely.

The college has accepted and refined on the habit of spasmodic driving for this and that hysterical purpose to the extent that it is not unknown for student periodicals to plead for a Go to Class Week; the editors at least are reaching for the ideal of the perfecting of the scholar.

VI

What is the net result to the graduates of a college where they have been instructed by specialists, driven for this and that spasmodic purpose, and have slept through pleas for "the higher things of life"? What do graduates of ten years know? What do they believe? In what direction are they moving? Do they swim sturdily toward some shore where "the higher things" rear their shining towers? Or do they lie on the stream, drifting with contemporary winds and tides, rudderless and compassless in the ocean mists?

Teachers like to think that the results of their labors are important. The larger portion of their salary comes in character dividends, so they are told by comfortable messengers from outside their quiet harbor. They want to believe it.

But can they? What do they see when alumni who have been playing this or that game in the outside maelstrom return for a new commencement?

There are a few exceptional swimmers, of course, most of whom are too intent on their goal to return to harbor. But the usual run of old grads are of two types. The larger squad are those who cannot swim, never could have learned to swim had their course of training been ten years instead of four. They are perfectly satisfied with their game and are as unctuous and vacuous in their devotion to "the higher things" which they have never glimpsed as their fellow drifters. There is food and drink in the ocean of life, there is plenty of plankton, there is salt spray and good companionship, there is *life*. Some of them trust piously in a good harbor at the end; some think nothing about the end, but only of the drifting; some pessimistically assert there is no harbor and what difference?

These successful drifters are a pathetic object of contemplation but they should not be a grievous one. They are as perfectly happy as their capacities admit. It may have been a questionable ethical procedure to accept their tuition money for four years, but they themselves loudly proclaim that they got their money's worth, and they should know.

It is the other group that brings dismay and terrible doubt to the teacher. They are swimmers; they can buck a tide; they had a glimpse in college of "the higher things." Their teachers had expected much of them and had made them specialists. They had seemed to know what it was all about when they were freshmen or even sophomores; but by the time of their graduation, they knew only dimly what it was *all* about, and knew partly what something was about. They had been great possibilities. However, when they got out into the current without a compass, though with a strong stroke, their horizon shut in close about them, "the higher things" veiled as to the others, they struck out for the visible objective. They were prepared for life, educated for life, finished products. Sometimes a commonplace phrase takes on a strange, occasionally a terrifying aspect, like the profile of a dear, well-known friend that a moment of intense vision renders bizarre. "Educated for life" thus sounds to me in a certain mood like "Sent to Stillwater for life." They knew what life had in store, what valuations they put upon various rewards, and had merely to swim along until the right reward came in sight, then pull hard for the shore, and be settled — for life. In ten years they are firmly rooted, in twenty years they are pillars of society who will never skirt the ocean's rims. They believe in old-fashioned morality for their children, try to induce them to read Charles Dickens' fifteen-dollar-a-word *Life of Our Saviour*, and still speak of "the higher things." But they are puzzled and dismayed by the rumors that come from the Russias and Chinas and Indias of the world of thought. They had prepared for the life of twenty years before, not for the life of today.

In short, they have imperfectly learned the meaning of unity. Time, a mere twenty years, has betrayed them. They knew, they had been told, what was the best twenty years ago. What they lacked was the will to learn and the technique to discover the best today, when they are mature, and twenty years hence, when they will be ripe.

VII

What is the proper purpose of a college? To prepare students for life? No! To unprepare them! To prepare them for what is not yet, but may be; some of which inevitably *will be* in spite of how many uneducated people exist, more of which *would be* if colleges prepared for the future instead of the present.

The great, bulky, cumbersome reptiles of the Mesozoic were well prepared for the conditions of their age, and much did they enjoy the lush life of their time. The scrawny little mammal ancestor of man, living precariously and dangerously out of reach of the lords of creation, had found hard sledding for thousands of years. But he had a biological premonition which the reptile had not, that he was living in a transition age. Times were changing and nature was educating man's ancestor in habits and tastes and aptitudes suited to the time to come. The saurian world was

14

emphasizing the wrong qualities, in the pleasant dream that life would go on in the same grooves. Man's ancestor was already something of a humanist, learning to take the long view, growing hair for the cold days to come, developing his arms and hands to enable him to reach "the higher things" and avoid the swamps and marshes where his lordly contemporaries ramped and bogged and left their bones for the future paleontologist.

VIII

It is fitting — almost inescapable to conclude with the words of the rarely beautiful man who was pastor for many years in the church across the campus, a man both of learning and of insight: "Not this or that," the Reverend Mr. Herbert Leonard used to say, "but both, and more."

The Encyclopedia Britannica tells us that the circle is easy to construct, though hard to compute. I must accept that authority, but with some mental reservations when I think of the integrative life, composed of its infinite number of tangential lines. Surely it is not easy to construct. But also surely it is difficult to compute its value to the individual and his world, for its value is as nearly infinite as its component and integrative parts.

Chaos-Cosmos Suite

THROUGH *the fourth decade my topic for the December meeting of Quill Club was monotonously the growing chaos on the earth. These verses recall something of the history of that period.*

1932   Chaos in the Cosmos,
              Comfort in the street;
              Christmas in the top-shops,
              Love on limping feet.

              Dearth for all the earth-born,
              Starvation for the soul.
              Death rides in Manchuria,
              Scoring goal on goal.

              Ramsay takes his pound of flesh
              To stay the sterling pound;
              Herbert searches substitutes
              To sand his slipping round.

              Dollars still are steady,
              Though harder now to find;
              Workers lean and ready,
              Bankers fat and blind.

              Gracious God in heaven,
              Where on earth is leaven?
              Nerve the arm, direct the mind
              To plan a course for humankind.

1936   Chaos in the Cosmos,
              Carnage throughout Spain;
              Drizzling over Madrid
              Falls a bloody rain.

Chaos in the Red Ranks!
What are Peoples' Fronts?
Crises make strange playmates,
Queer, bewildered stunts.

World areek with puzzles,
Crossword and acrostic.
News-sheets needing muzzles,
Sentiments, a caustic.

Chaos in the Cosmos,
Hell and Empyrean.
Everything in Limbo
Worth a limber bean.

1937   Chaos in the New Deal!
Hand over Uncle Sam
To Economic Royalists
Who do not give a picayune?

Or move a bit to Left,
Say at least we nudge it
By levying on Capital
And balancing the budget?

Chaos in the Cosmos,
Christmas gone to pot!
What was not has come to pass,
Whatever was, is not.

1938   Chaos in the Aryan Reich,
Bitter, blond, and blind,
No place left in Germany
For Jew — or humankind.

Japan's jazzed-up juggernaut
Rolling over Han.
Flame can singe but not consume
Phoenix heart of man.

17

Chaos covers North Star,
No longer sailor's guide.
Business thunders on the right;
Reaction's on the tide.

Chaos in geography,
Cosmos among friends!
In the soul's topography
Love still governs ends.

1939   Chaos and Cosmos went out together,
Went out to pick a bone.
Between them hardly the weight
    of a feather . . .
Chaos came back alone.

1940   Total War and Chaos
By sprite and nymph and gnome.
Albion in Albania Land
Aims the Greece that once was Glory
At the Rome that once was Grand.

Total War and Chaos,
Special pleas galore.
What besides her life
Is Albion fighting for?
What is fighting for?

What can we say for Christmas in this Year
Of Grace? If "grace" can be assigned indeed
To Nineteen Forty? *Year of Our Lord* also
Betrays a tone of grim burlesque. Burlesque
For Past and dire presage for Future. Is
Next year to mark the coming of the Lord?
Is this a year of final grace
Upon the end of which our nation's God
Shall force a reckoning?
Have we so soon run past the debt date?

Not to the swift nor strong, but victory
Will rest upon the deep and laboring lungs,
The steady, steadfast heart, the steely will.

And love will help. Nay, love may drop a bomb,
For depth and lateral displacement will
Explode the submarines of greed and hate
Out of the sea where swims the life of man.

To say a mass for Christ? Or tender friends
Reciprocative gifts? Small Christmas there!
Love in a church, or home, avoiding wolves
That ravine in the street and market place,
Camps, factories, fields, and laboratories crammed
With germs of civil war, grand suicide,
Avoiding every chance of testing love
Before the brutal body blows inflame
The passions and befog the brain?

                              No, no,
Dear God, you gave intelligence to man,
Grant him the wit to ask her sister, love!

1941   We spoke of Cosmos, Chaos,
          A dozen years or more;
          And now comes Cosmos-Chaos
          Rat-tat-ting at the door.

          For Cosmos has been Chaos,
          Peace, masked and breeding war.
          Now Chaos must bear Cosmos,
          As Cosmos Chaos bore.

          One speaks of Chaos-Cosmos,
          The game at even score.
          ABCD and Axis
          Line up at Singapore.

          (Written on the morning of December 7, 1941.)

19

Educing and Traducing

SOME REMARKS ON EDUCATION AND TREASON

ENGAGED in the strenuous business of living we have too little time to think how we ought to live. In the daily stampede from east to west only the genius, who feels rather than reasons out his mission, can be quite sure he is traveling in the direction he desires. When a man drops out along the way to orientate himself, the lusty cavalcade sweeps on out of sight and the chagrinned loiterer must then either take the dust in the beaten track, always behind the procession, or, should he become convinced that his way lies not there but here, strike out through untrodden waste and tangled jungle with no guide but his own puzzled compass.

So it comes about that *right* and *wrong* are emasculated words in our performance. We take our stereotyped copy of the play, tragedy, farce, or seriocomedy, and content ourselves with furniture shifting, choosing our make-up, perhaps even a variation in the words to relieve monotony. But that is all. What we shall do is outlined; how we shall do it is entrusted partly to our discretion provided we do not depart too widely from conventional acting. Thus we fill our mouths with "practical" and "expedient," a mess of pottage for which we barter our birthright, saying what and what not.

However the desire to say *what* sometimes conquers fear, and the humble actor is emboldened to turn critic. If I may change the figure, one learns to examine the very pedestal on which he stands; he hammers the stones in the founda-

NOTE. First published in the *Forum*, June 1913.

20

tion of his creed of living, if so be there is any rotten material or false corner in its construction. Society warns him that if he tries to be a little Samson, he will be buried in the ruins. But perhaps he may escape under a protecting beam. Society urges him not to try lifting himself by his own bootstraps. But if the boots are paper-soled, he may pull the bottoms out, discard the tops and leap the better.

If we may believe Mark Twain's version of the early history of Eden, it was only a few days after creation that our first mother, pointing to an awkward, self-conscious-looking bird, said, "Ooh Adam, look at the dodo!" The father of the race stopped scratching "with a stick in the mold" long enough to scratch his shaggy poll and ask, "Why do you call it a dodo, my dear?" Eve was puzzled, but only for a moment. "Why, because it *looks* like a dodo," said she with a pert toss of her pretty head. It was now Adam's turn for puzzlement, but after an admiring glance at Eve, he admitted that it *did* look like a dodo — and so was made the first proselyte.

A sort of unwitting romantic chivalry wrought our first father's downfall; but we lack his excuse for our enhancement of the offense. Dogma, aggression, and arrogance on the one hand, ignorance, indolence, and servility on the other, make the proselytizer and the proselyte.

Mr. G. K. Chesterton is a suggestive writer. You either agree with him heartily or differ more heartily. When he told us *What's Wrong with the World* he had my enthusiastic assent until he came to education, which to him is anathema. First he says that it is nothing and then that it is treason. He writes with fine scorn of the pedants who pretend that they can teach something they do not know, can give something they do not have. The impression one gets from the book is that the author could go out any time on the Strand and buy a pennyworth of education — if he had something to put it in. Some of it, he would admit, might be worm-eaten and some only shells, for you must take your chances as you do with chestnuts. And of course it is just as well to know the dealer. He is even liberal enough to detect a slight quality difference between the kind of education which the reader of *Prizy Bits* gets and that which is injected into the Rhodes Scholar at hundreds of pounds a year. But the notion of *educing*, drawing out by suggestion powers individual to a student, is to him a joke, a pedantic hoax. A teacher must teach something: rule of three, vertical writing, shorthand, Swedish movement, aviation, anything; and to teach the rule of three he must feel confident that three times three is nine; he must be willing and anxious to suffer martyrdom in the cause. In short all education is dogma; nothing but dogma educates.

A similar idea of education was advanced by my little niece. Newly instructed in things academic from the viewpoint of the grades, she asked me how big my "pupils" were. When I told her they were grown up, some of them taller than I, she was fairly stunned, and could only exclaim, lapsing for the moment into natural grammar, "What! Don't they know nothing?" To be six feet tall and uneducated was an intellectual poser to her. Similarly to Chesterton there were no uneducated people in England; that is, everyone has somehow had something beaten into his head.

Dogma has no place in the philosophy of Protestantism, however large it has been written in her history. When Paul, the first Protestant, "conferred not with flesh and blood" after his conversion, but instead of visiting Peter and the other leaders in Jerusalem retired into the wilderness for a season, and returned to preach his own revelation, he created a philosophy that has destroyed much of his own dogma. He was sowing a magnificent seed whose vitality he himself never completely sensed.

Paul shattered one dogma, but set up another; and the new was nearly or altogether as rigid as the old. So also

Emerson, who helped to free the mind of the nineteenth century. "Insist on yourself; never imitate" was the noble lesson that he taught a timid, plagiaristic America. Thoreau took up the echo and his flute in *Walden* gave back, "When one man honestly believes in an unpopular measure, it is already in a majority of one." One slight shift enabled Emerson to arrive at his definition of genius: "To believe your own thought, to believe that what is true for you is true for all men — that is genius." Perhaps! But that is also the destruction of genius. Napoleon believed that, and had he not so confided in his own suzerainty it might have gone differently with him both in his lifetime and on the page of history. He could not understand that "France was not the world, and that he was not all France." And his was but one of the fiascoes resulting from the failure to appreciate that not all others are bending reeds or flimsy willows.

This form of megalomania is a result of Emerson's doctrine "carried into Africa." Insistence on self is worth teaching, but we have learned it too well. At least we have learned the obverse; but the reverse, there's the rub. The knife cuts both ways. The hiltless dagger wounds the hand that guides it. What of others? When did they forfeit their divine right? Why, when they stopped agreeing with us, of course, for then they forsook truth and gave up the trade of genius. We may call upon Emerson again, and often under the spell of his inspired sophisms we feel the glow of a valid title to genius if we only succeed in contradicting ourselves. The number of weak-kneed, double-jointed principles that have taken refuge behind "a foolish consistency is the hobgoblin of little minds" is legion. They hide their heads, but leave their other absurd extremities exposed to every curious eye.

The warning of Jesus goes unheeded: "Woe unto you, hypocrites, ye compass sea and land to make one proselyte." To win a convert by educating him, by legitimate appeal to his whole mental life, is entirely laudable; but to float a proselyte over a bar of intellectual indifference or prejudice on a momentary froth of feeling, leaving him when the tide ebbs stranded on a barren reef empty of spiritual significance, there to struggle and flounder in helpless despair — this, I imagine, was the object of the Master's denunciation. You may have seen the foolish, vacant, abashed look of the victim of some strolling hypnotist when awakened from the trance in which he had been wildly applauding a baseball game or boxing an imaginary opponent around the stage. So the proselyte looks when asked for the reason of the faith within him; so no doubt looked Adam when little Cain asked him later why the bird looked like a dodo; and so look all we brother and sister dupes after the political or religious mountebank has moved on.

Those well grounded in philosophy will be thinking, "Nevertheless Emerson was right. One must accept one's own judgments before there is any possibility of reasoning." But remember the judgments of the other man. You must accept them before there is any possibility of conclusions.

Our senses are notorious deceivers. When the perceptions of a number of others contradict or fail to confirm our own, we are led to wonder, unless we too have some form of megalomania, whether we have not been the victims of illusion. Who does not remember how the roistering doctor and his crowd of hoodlums in *Handy Andy* got the apothecary drunken, and on his awakening solemnly assured him that he was dead, killed by O'Grady's beating; that he had been revived and was only temporarily sustained by the magic of the new power of galvanism, which he had presumed to belittle on the previous evening. And when they showed him the great welts on his body, painted with bootblacking and cabbage water, the poor fellow, though now sober and feeling very painfully alive, gave himself up for dead and turned his face to the wall. Subtract from mankind

24

the blind and nearsighted and astigmatic, the deaf and the hard of hearing, the paralytics and the quasi-paralyzed, the de-olfactoried and the de-gustatized — and few will remain to render perfect testimony of the senses. In sense perception then we have learned to profit by our limitations; when two or three friends assure me that what I call red is green to them, I conclude I am color-blind.

In normal life we are told that we do not strictly forget anything; yet we know that we do mislay facts so outrageously that when someone else finds them, we have difficulty in recognizing them even as casual acquaintances.

How is it in matters of taste, esthetic and moral? "De gustibus non est disputandum" is quoted by many and heeded by next to none. When ten men love what I hate, I am bound theoretically at least to admit that the ten have right of way. I may not believe that the mere majority is always right; in fact I may hold that the majority is usually wrong. Still in the face of the multitudes who think Goethe a very great poet, I have no business to flaunt my unsupported heresy; nor considering the all but universally distributed fondness for religious ritual, should I seriously oppose my distaste. Of course I may occupy a unique position on these or on any subject and may regard with indifference the tastes of all the world; at the same time I should be all the calendared kinds of fool if I tried to substitute my vagary, my bias, my prejudice for the combined approval of mankind.

> We all surmise,
> They this thing and I that;
> Whom shall my soul believe?

We know that we are deluded, have erroneous beliefs. We follow after false fires, will-o'-the-wisps that never come close and have no reality. We begin with a thorough persuasion of ghosts, and end skeptical even of spiritism; we begin firmly convinced of fairies and end not so sure even of angels. Illusions, elusions, delusions; perversions of sense, memory, taste, and belief — it requires a very slight inductive advance to the acknowledgment that our conceptions and fundamental postulates, even our sacred intuitions themselves, the perception of the *Ding an sich* if there be such, may prove false. In a lecture on immortality William James made a suggestive remark on the nature of the brain. He likened it to an imperfect curtain which lets Soul through in a more or less modified form; and again to a transmitting and refracting medium which admits just certain rays of the universal Soul. Even though this suppositional ocean of Soul at the background of the world, from which flow and to which ebb the individual souls of men and women, may not satisfy your philosophic needs, the figure is nonetheless valuable. It is in the nature of all matter to be imperfect. Every brain has some flaw which mars and distorts what we call axioms of thought as much as the astigmatic lens of the eye distorts visual images.

If we are sensible enough to recognize the disorders of a stomach that rejects as offensive what others enjoy, or the defects of a crystalline lens, or the exaggerated tinglings of a raw nerve, why should we stubbornly insist that the distortions produced by another physical part, the cortex of the brain, have the peculiar approval of Providence?

The bearings of all this are clear enough, I suppose. In religion, politics, and ordinary intercourse we are engaged in the work of traduction, not education; instead of teachers and learners, we have evolved by our fundamental axioms of thought a society of proselytizers and proselytes. Any assumption not our own we regard as eccentric and make little effort to understand sympathetically. We play like children a never-ending game of "Fox in the Morning," striving for a few proselytes to begin with, and when we have made them, they become "ten-fold more the children of hell than ourselves" and engage more zealously in the capture of others. We are deaf men with big voices, who instead of getting ear trumpets get megaphones. He who blares the loudest establishes his assumptions and fills his platform with proselytes. Occasionally there is a voice heard whose modulation and sweet reasonableness penetrates the din. Happily sometimes a healthy instinct gains control and the throng rushes to find the prophet. But alas, when they have surrounded him, their strident summoning to renewed proselytism drowns the voice and dogma reigns again.

The church is a great if not *the* great offender. Even before and incessantly since Charlemagne baptized and later beheaded his five thousand converts, one method or another of proselytizing has been in vogue. As a boy of eleven I had a season of sleeplessness induced by the horrible pictures stamped upon my imagination by a minister of the gospel. It was the Last Day in the final conflagration of the world, and I saw myself, a little charred imp, running here and there over the shriveled earth, stumbling against seared, overtaken sinners and striving vainly to hide from the wrath of God. Maybe that was the only way to stop my shooting sparrows with an air gun or to secure an ungrumbling attendance at three Sunday services, but I still think that such usurpation of the vivid and nascent imagination of youth is one of the more insidious types of hypnotism.

A surprisingly large number of students who come from orthodox Christian homes develop a flippant cynicism or something like a small pretentious atheism. Doubtless a variety of causes enters into their composition, but beyond question many of them have been preached into skepticism. As children they have listened to canting phrases in pulpit and home, and their budding reason has often been met by an arbitrary fiat. They are in revolt not so much against religion as against the treason of the proselytizer.

In an election year no candidate seems bold enough to

understand any of his opponents. A national political campaign could be an educational experience. That it is not is indicated by the relatively slight increase from one election to the next in the popular vote. Apparently many simple men and women are so bulldozed this way and that, by every "progressive" candidate and editorial writer, that they remain on the safe side by staying at home on election day. Campaign speeches and campaign literature have as real an educational value as the yells of rival colleges at a football game. In politics education comes nearer to treason than in any other area of life.

What of the learned world of scholars and experts? Surely here one should expect to find the calm and honest pursuit of knowledge and wisdom. The scientist will not be dogmatic; the metaphysician will withhold judgment; the authority in any field will wait until all the returns are in. Does he? Do they? It seems absurd, but the technologist is frequently your greatest dogmatist, and the expert, most skilled in selection of evidence in support of his hobby. For proof listen to the sociologists and economists in "Town Meeting of the Air," to the philosophers and pundits on the "University of Chicago Round Table," and to the political scientists and literary critics in the excellent "Invitation to Learning." Religious dogma can but declare you unsaved; how much more depressing when scientific dogma dismisses you as uninformed or artistic dogma as uncultured.

Turn finally to the vast field of human intercourse, to the *vox pop*. The charge has been often made that Americans never converse or discuss; they merely argue. Were argument ideal the charge would not be condemnatory; but the ordinary course of argument is something like this: unwarranted assumptions on each side, neither agreed to nor even noticed by the other, charges and countercharges, criminations and recriminations, iterations and reiterations. Langland described it beautifully in the *Vision of Piers Plowman* — not an American poem, it may be observed:

28

"Thou liest" and "thou liest" leapt out at ones
And either hit other under the cheke.

That is the natural method of argument. Everyone knows
the fallacies — how to beg the question, evade the issue,
shift ground, and all the rest. Few distinguish the solidity
of logic from the quicksands of illogic; and even the *no-
blesse*, those who should *oblige*, college debaters for instance, use their knowledge of logic in steering as close to
the wind as they safely can, for their aim is victory. That is,
they are preparing for the tortuous law and the labyrinth of
business. In America and elsewhere most discussion is argument, most argument is war, and everyone knows what war
is.

There is a trite old saying about a man convinced against
his will. He remains of the same opinion still because he has
not been educated, he has been betrayed. He has not been
appealed to on his own grounds, but has been bullied in a
strange field. His particular divine right has been trampled
underfoot. When bested in argument he is merely cha-
grined, not convinced; and his thought is not at all on how
to gain benefit from his new knowledge, but on how to gain
skill to outflank his conqueror.

Take a salient illustration — what I believe to be the most
obstructive and dangerous intolerance of modern times.
Certainly few fanaticisms of the Middle Ages were less intelligent, and not even our stupid color prejudices are so obstructive.

The Christian church is founded upon the ideal of brotherhood. The millenium toward which sincere Christians are
straining is a state of society where the Golden Rule shall
have become a working principle. Christians hope for and
profess to aim at a utopian condition of society in which it
will be possible for each actually to put the welfare of others on a par with his own. Some few well-meaning, blind
folk say they are able to do this now, and perhaps a negligible fraction of the salt of the earth are, without making

any such pretensions, actually doing it. Yet the overwhelming testimony of honest observers of life, who like to turn full face to the truth, is that in a society as at present organized in most parts of the world, saturated with individualism and goaded at all points by competition, the Golden Rule is a piece of sentimentalism impossible of fullfilment. It has no workability in trade. No businessman could actually practice the Golden Rule for six months without going into bankruptcy. And while we are not all businessmen, the income of every worker is so related to the pervasive genius of our time, "business," that we dare not call our souls wholly our own.

This is the situation that both laymen and clergy unite in deploring while in the same breath they assent to their bonds, hoping for release only after long ages of gradual filing. At times they appear actually contented that business abounds, since there is likely to be such a long season for grace to "much more abound." It never occurs to them that they themselves are the judges and jailers and might accomplish their freedom in much less than a million years. So the church, well meaning but shackled; puzzled but submissive and inert.

Socialism also claims the ideal of brotherhood. For more than half a century this protoplasmic germ has fought its way along, through, and around incalculable prejudice, frothing here and there with ignorant fanaticism, unwisely and irrelevantly fuming at realities sometimes, tilting at windmills, performing hara-kiri out of sheer spite, committing all the absurdities to be expected of a new and vital thought let loose in the world. New, did I say? Certainly not that. The heart of socialism is a simple, naive faith in the brotherhood of man, along with a consuming passion to realize it. The socialist is a man who really believes something and insists like a maniac on acting according to his belief.

A simple-minded Martian who knew nothing of earthly intolerance and proselytizing would expect to see two such forces as the church and socialism unite for the common cause. What a deadening shock to the Martian when he discovered the actual state of affairs, the majority of organized socialists and the majority of organized Christians with drawn daggers trying either to convert in Charlemagne style or to exterminate each other.

All men of good will believe in brotherhood. But the church insists on conversion, soul regeneration, raising each brother singly—which is sound doctrine. Change the human heart, says the Christian, and all evil will cease. Socialism demands that we raise a million brothers at a time. Better the material conditions of living, render economic justice, and give the human hearts of the toilers a chance to expand. "Raise the individual!" "Raise Society!" cry these good men. But each thinks the other is only trying to raise the devil. The church adores the Saviour, and socialism adores the world He came to save; neither tries to educate, each to traduce; one blatantly impeaches motives, the other eloquently deplores methods.

Now the strength of the church is world-old, and the insistence on the revivifying of the individual is founded on a rock. Socialism is newer, but the right of society to profit by the collective brawn and brain, and the validity of the claim that better things will assist to better souls, is also strongly based. Jesus did not concern himself with economic propaganda, but when he did touch upon the economic order, as in the parable of the laborers in the vineyard, he was decidedly socialistic.

When will honest socialists and honest Christians learn to recognize the good will in each, cease perverting each other's doctrine and begin understanding it; quit fighting for proselytes and begin the work of education? When they do, the world will listen and agree with their joint decision.

Tolerance has always marked the method of the great teachers. Socrates took men on their own premises, and led them to his conclusions, making them feel all the while that they themselves were directing the route and determining the destination. He knew the necessity of being fair to the other man's assumptions and logic from the purely utilitarian standpoint of one who himself had a propagandum. He conceded a man was right in order to prove him wrong.

Epictetus enunciated the justice of tolerance. Not only the *must*, but the *ought*. How can it be otherwise? I am one of a billion; my opinion is one of a hundred million — but a unit in the universal ballot; and so when the barbarous lash cut and maimed him, he bowed his head to the persecutor, murmuring, "It seems so to him."

Jesus who is called the Christ, knowing the didactic value of tolerance as well as Socrates, feeling the justice of it as well as Epictetus, more than these eternally glorifies the beauty of it in his "Judge not that ye be not judged," in his "Neither do I condemn thee," in his "Do unto others . . ." which among many has one special meaning: *Have respect for your neighbor's opinion as you have respect for your own.*

In opinion there should be survival of the fittest, but fittest must not be identified with strongest. The fittest will never be determined by vilification and a trial of lungs; it will grow out of a sympathetic understanding. The combined good will in man is stronger than aught else; it can prevail against the gates of hell. But it must be assembled in the light to be effective; in the twilight of mutual distrust it cannot distinguish friend from foe, and instead of marching triumphantly to the goal fritters the time away in demanding credentials. Learners are more in demand than teachers. And as for dogma, it betrays him that gives and him that takes.

Paradox

"Boys are boys," the cautious teacher
Carps, inculcates, drones, and drills;
"As you are, we were before you,
Ours the stuff your bosom fills;
You repeat us, tone and feature,
We have felt your jejune thrills."

"Men are men, and will be never
Angels," smile the ironist and sage;
"Evolution's slain its billions;
Men are men now, age on age.
Why this boyish green endeavor
Million-year-old bonds to sever
In unsophisticated rage?
        Why not just be realistic,
        Ironistic, eulogistic
        Of man's changeless heritage?"

"We are busy with our dreaming,"
Cry the dear, dream-giddy boys.
"Boys are men and men are angels;
Take your middle-agéd toys —
We will learn if this our gleaming
Vision be not all a-teeming
With some future solid joys.
Run along and mix your gruel;
Irony just adds more fuel
To our fire. Don't rouse our ire!
Go on writing pretty whimsy,

33

Subtle, cynical, and flimsy;
'Twill amuse you while we work
On the problems that you shirk."

March 27, 1927

(first published in the *Mid-West Student*)

A PRICKLY PINFEATHER

Enough of foolish harsh debate!
It sounds like hate.
Inverted love
Engenders strife and poisons life
As lilies fester into deep decay.

Enough of setting friends to rights,
Or maybe venting spites!
A cool disinterest
Masks the cold egotist.
Pure motives, shut from sunlight
And denied the proper mold for roots,
Are white and brittle as potato shoots.

Distrust the masochist!
He is your saddest Sadist at the core.

March 12, 1940

Partnership in Teaching English

FOR about fifty years American colleges have been trying seriously to teach English composition. Before that period students studied it. Probably it is just because the English departments have taken themselves so seriously that the subjects have so persistently refused to consider them so; and cynical journalists have found them such howling farces. At any rate there has not been a year of the half century of intensive English teaching when it has not been indicted in the press.

It used to be charged that the colleges, with all this new emphasis on composition, should turn out a greater number of literary prodigies. This was frequently heard in the sterile period of reconstruction after the Civil War and re-echoed nearly to the end of the century. But gradually the suspicion grew that this "soft impeachment" argued some softness in the head of the impeacher. Then the attack shifted. It was declared that the colleges did not even teach grammar and the rudiments of syntax. Students have been found guilty of all degrees of crimes against the language, from petty larceny and ordinary assault to murder in the first degree.

These criticisms are not so raucously uttered as formerly. It is pretty generally recognized that if the English departments have not produced any geniuses, they have not notoriously discouraged them, most of the poets and fictionists of the last two decades having struggled up through the handicaps of a college education. Also, not many fair-minded critics are disposed to blame the colleges severely for the too common barbarous grammar used by those who have

NOTE. First published in the *Educational Review*, June 1922.

secured a "pass" in English. If a high school graduate says he "ain't got no time for English," it is quite likely he will be saying the same thing when he is a college freshman, though he may not write it in a theme. It is a very young dog indeed who can learn new tricks in grammar; the college freshman is usually too old to make over his colloquial wardrobe.

But although the college may be freed from complicity in the crimes of solecism, English departments are themselves keenly sensitive to a fundamental derangement of their carefully planned efforts to teach composition. It is undeniable that college students, with some shining exceptions, not only are not literary artists, not only show occasional grammatical lapses, but, what is the vital thing, they cannot express themselves. Not a few seniors, those who have taken some English courses above the freshman year as well as those who have not, are unable to construct a clear outline of a developed theme and follow it through rigorously. Many more of them are unable to write "I" followed by anything not ponderous or banal; most of them are restricted to newspaper bromides and the technical slang of their major subjects. The question I raise is this. Who sinned — these students, the English department, or the assigners of papers in other college departments, where their major work lay? As an English teacher and a humanitarian, of course I lay the blame on the last and would hereinafter present my grounds.

A college junior or senior, carrying five subjects, is likely to have two or three courses selected from the following departments: history, philosophy, psychology, economics, education, political science, and sociology. He may or may not have a course in composition as well, but he is always asked to do a great deal of written work in connection with any of the subjects above, as well as in literature courses. It has come about recently that in several of these departments, notably in history and philosophy, where the lecture method is most in vogue, grades are almost wholly determined by quizzes and by one to four or more papers, in which the student regurgitates the material of the lectures, or makes brief summaries of books or chapters he has read in the library. Not infrequently it happens that a student is asked to do more writing in connection with a course in philosophy or history than is expected of him in an English course taken concurrently, and I believe that it is a rare exception to find an instructor who has the time or inclination (some possibly lack the qualifications) to call attention to anything but mistakes of fact. Many papers, sad to relate, are given the most cursory once-over; some, I suspect, do not fare so well. Quizzes at best are always laboratories of poor composition. Instructors are looking for the goods, and if it is delivered they do not scrutinize the form of the package. Beyond requiring accuracy of fact and condensation, it is probably undesirable to demand formal excellence. However, I speak particularly of the thesis prepared outside of the classroom.

It is not my purpose to decry the methods of teaching practiced in departments whose particular problems I know very little about. Indeed I am convinced that the "paper" evil is a necessary one in a great many lecture courses. But I am recording facts and viewing them with alarm. I know that much of the slovenly, unimaginative composition produced by college juniors and seniors is due neither to commissions nor omissions of the English department. I also have the particular grievance that when I ask for a moderate amount of writing that shows some personality, I get shocking revelations of fagged minds, drugged by the frequent necessity of warming over stale goods in other courses. Composition is a habit of mind and grows by what it feeds on. A student cannot well serve two masters, and he must get grades. In producing practical papers, he clogs the avenues of self-expression; in serving the brass Baal of fact he must inevitably lose touch with Jehovah, unless —

What is the answer? Two remedies only seem possible: either the instructors who require papers must teach composition, or there must be a correlation of the work in their departments with that of the English. The first is perhaps not a possible remedy at all; certainly not unless the teaching staff is increased beyond the limits of the feasible for the ordinary college. Some initial instruction might be given on the preparation of history papers (no doubt *is* given), but to render constructive assistance to a hundred freshmen, and then make corrections and suggestions for rewriting, is beyond the physical powers of an instructor who has several other courses in history to conduct.

What can be done on the second tack? It is as absurd to expect super-teachers of English as of history. Yet intelligent criticism must know substance as well as form; form as well as substance. If an English teacher shot a student who brought him an oration or a paper with the request to help him "whip it into shape" and pay no heed to the content, any jury of peers would return a verdict of justifiable homicide. However, English teachers cannot modestly enjoin omniscience in the service of their profession, and so it would seem that they must recognize this situation as an impasse. Not absolutely!

Already the English teacher more than any other regards all knowledge as his province. He is not often the master of any other field of knowledge, but he tries to get a bird's-eye view of many, and if he is a good teacher of English, he is at least partly successful. It should be demanded as part of the recognized training of the teacher of composition that he should show fitness in basic courses in many other departments; indeed, the writing he himself requires makes it imperative that he have a great deal of general knowledge of a fundamental sort. Successful teachers of English have found that they must profess *der Allerleiwissenschaft.* Perhaps scholars in other fields have been too much inclined to ridicule this pretension (though of course in many instances the pretension has been sufficiently ridiculous), but the theory is sound. A critic must first of all know something. There is no more vicious dualism than the assumption that a man can advise how to say something he does not understand. Let the requirements be stiffened for those who aim to teach English. The result will be that more of the very best intellects will be attracted to this field; in fact, it will be the most attractive field to those who combine in their tastes a passion for knowledge with a passion for expression.

Given an English faculty of the type indicated, the impasse would disappear; the problem could be handled in a variety of ways. The simplest would be for the teachers of composition to devote themselves almost solely to the writing required by the other departments. For instance, the history instructor, after reading his papers, would turn them over to the professor of English with a statement of the purpose the paper was supposed to have; the latter would return it to the student with suggestions, who, after reading and working upon these, would hand the revised paper back to the history instructor, who would then record a final grade based upon his own standards. The English instructor has made a record meanwhile on the same piece of work, based upon the ideals of such writing that he has been holding up to the student in composition. In this way, although it might happen that the history instructor demands primarily soundness of fact and view, and the English instructor demands effectiveness of form, the student will feel that composition is a unit; the false double standard will disappear. If these papers could then be reduced to a minimum, not more than one or two at most a semester, permitting the student to devote more time to composition of a more general character, to develop his observation, his narrative skill, or ease and audacity in the more personal forms of writing, there would be a new heaven and a new earth, and they would be the same.

THE ARTS OF TIME

The arts of time! Dear God, when time is not,
When over us eternity comes down,
Shall all their lovely ministry, forgot,
Lie frozen mute, and timeless, tideless, drown?

Ah let us but take poetry along,
And make the time as finite as may be,
Unless immortal life can nourish song,
As well the hangman's cap . . . Eternity!

1938

Anagramania

Anyone who writes *prose* well
Knows the *ropes* and rings the bell.

If one has but a little nerve,
And can't write prose, a *verse* will *serve*.

The poet's rolling eye is bent on
A mission for a *sonnet* to be *sent on*.

A type of realistic modernist
Confuses *art* with *tar,* and will insist
That feathers add a too romantic touch.
Therefore plain tar will serve his every twist.

To sense a poet may sometimes be hard;
It may be *drab*'s the color of a *bard.*

In some good words you can't alter a letter;
Never hope to change for a better.
If a love *song* you make *gosn,* or *nogs,* or *snog,*
You do not deserve to get her.

There once was a lady who cried in the beer,
A drink more fitting denied her.
Had she been an anagrammatist,
She would have *cried* in the *cider.*

How potent the apostrophe
In criminal reform can be!
If you write "man" and put it after
Manslaughter changes to *man's laughter.*

Word-mongers all are gently damned:
In *a grandma* they're *anagram'd.*

1942

41

Reading or Riding – Which Way?

SHORTLY after returning to America from a year in the Orient I went into a favorite bookstore and inquired of an old acquaintance, "How's business?" His reply is a classic: "Not very good. Nobody readin'; everybody ridin'." This jolted a recent sojourner in the more or less serene East all the more sharply because just that morning the home-town paper had reported four deaths from week-end motor accidents, the news was still hot about the loss of two great naval planes hopping from Honolulu to San Francisco, and the same week was to culminate catastrophe when a great dirigible on its way to the Minnesota State Fair was snuffed out in flame and twisted into a mass of charnel junk.

It seems to be a fair and debatable question to ask whether America is reading or riding.

To begin, let us excommunicate certain activities and passivities that sail under false colors.

1. *First-grade reading.* The passing of the eye back and forth across the printed page; inhaling words and exhaling them again; newspaper reading; headline reading; the kind of thing the boy did who spelled out, "Here-is-a-worm-do-not-tread-on-it," and with a few faulty vowels and a misplaced accent made it, "Here is a warm doughnut. Tread on it."

Reading at its worst is a miracle, not far behind the first and greatest of creation. The communication of one mind with another, first by sounds for the present moment and then by marks and scratches on bark, papyrus, wax, parchment, paper, for distant places and far-off times, is a matter

NOTE. Abstract from the *Methodist Review*, September 1928.

42

for never-ceasing wonder. But, after all, only the beginning of the reading adventure, this alphabetic reading.

2. *Topical reading.* The reading of textbooks and sources collateral to some course, with a view to acquire information to be embalmed in a notebook or regurgitated in a quiz. Sit down in a college library, with a book hypocritically opened before you, and furtively watch the busy students doing their "collateral" (perhaps so named because it is considered a security against scholastic disaster). This is what you see at every table, for the technique is the same for the conscientious coed and the flippant flapper alike, although the latter may enjoy more interruptions to admire and be admired. The student seated stolidly and squarely, fountain pen in right hand, hovering over a loose-leaf notebook; under the left forearm and elbow a volume, one of those listed on the reference sheets on the wall, the left hand skillfully manipulating the pages; a steady artesian well of pure information rising to the eye from the book on the left and passing down through the good right arm and the fountain pen to the book on the right. Perhaps the mind occasionally acts as a reinforcing station, but not often; there are usually excellent connections and no waits between afferent and efferent trains. The operatives of the brain have developed a high efficiency in sending out incoming freight with no loss of time whatever, and the weighty matter of the sources is transferred to the ink line and deposited in the note warehouse, still in the original packages, though sometimes sadly marred by rapid handling. Here and there, happy to relate, is one who seems by his look of curious inquiry to be unwrapping the paragraphs and examining their contents, perhaps even classifying and pigeonholing and relabeling before sending along the revised shipment. But the system of quantity transfer does not permit much of this amateurish curiosity. *Anathema maranatha!*

3. *Pastime reading.* Recreational (not re-creational) reading; soaking up a story tonight which tomorrow night will have evaporated and made place for another absorbing tale in which a bored mind loses itself. This is not so much reading as a genteel kind of suicide. We are killing our time, which is our life. A mind tired out by severe labor may profitably eclipse itself thus willfully for a time, because on such a mind the eclipse is sure to pass. But the tragedy of so much pastime reading is that its devotees have never developed the capability of anything better; continually lulled by opiates, the dreamer never learns that a wholesome stimulant like Carlyle or Thoreau or Shaw can sting him into life, releasing dormant energies of soul which are aching for exercise.

It were foolish to cry out against this possibly fallowing pastime — losing the self serves its own useful purposes — but let us recognize it for what it is. "He who would lose his life, the same shall find it" has small truth in the realm of reading. He who would lose his life permanently can discover no better method than to lose it night after night in romantic lullabies.

These types of elementary or of prostitute reading aside, what *is* reading?

Only *creative* reading is reading. Creative reading is the soul of the writer plus the soul of the reader.

Let me make my meaning clear by a few practical precepts:

1. Try to understand the author's purpose. The author is host; the reader, guest. Ordinary courtesy requires that the guest wait for the host to disclose the object of the invitation before presuming to dissent. Running off in the middle of the soup is a light offense compared with shutting the book after the first ten pages with the conviction that there is nothing in it we want. We are judging ourselves, not the book.

2. Try to like the book. It might be said of all good books as of a certain great writer, "You must first love him ere to you he will seem worthy of your love." In a sense we can never understand anything unless we love it. Without sympathy we shall always stand outside the gate, for the portals of literature bear the legend, "All ye who enter here must first cast indifference, callousness, antipathy, hate, aside." It is hard even to pity the modern who ignores Homer and Milton; the social reformer who patronizingly dismisses Charles Lamb, or the intellectual who scorns all the American Victorians. The creative reader is catholic in his tastes; he cries, "All good things are mine." If he must confine himself either to the books he likes and agrees with, or to the books he dislikes and disagrees with, he will choose the latter, for then his soul will not vegetate.

3. Learn to follow your curiosities.* Curiosity is to reading what hunger is to eating. It does us a little, but not much good to eat what we do not want; so it does us a little but not much good to read what we feel no curiosity about. Some qualification is necessary here, of course, else we could never advance from lower to higher interests. It is possible, though not easy, to develop curiosity for classics which at first do not attract in comparison with the watery pulp that may have blighted our early tastes. Still if Plato does not at first attract us, we may well have some curiosity to discover what others find in him — to learn why there has been such a remarkable prejudice in his favor. The low motive in morality, fear of punishment, for instance, may lead to a higher type of conscience-guided conduct; so the fear of ostracism from the ranks of cultured people has sometimes led literary Philistines to gain an honest, personal curiosity in the masters.

4. Never ignore a curiosity in reading. When the mind starts under its own power never choke it off in order to go

*I am indebted to J. B. Kerfoot's suggestive book, *How To Read.*

45

on with the story or discussion. Let it lead where it will until it becomes evident that the tank is empty. Or, to wrench violently to another figure, run the rabbit to its burrow. Don't stop until the scent is lost; this is our rabbit and our hunt; the book can wait; this curious scent may never come again. If "Markheim" starts us off on our quest, let us shut the book until we are no longer interested in and by ourselves. If the editorial lets drop a significant hint, let us shake it by the ears and hold on to it like a bull terrier until we have examined it as minutely as is possible with our experience or understanding or vision. This is the reason "Markheim" and the newspaper exist for us.

Is the book true? Not unless our experience helps us to verify and accept it. Is it false? Why is it false, and what is the truth? In this way the false thing can become the vehicle of the best truth we have at our disposal. So all roads lead to Rome. So all books let our souls out to explore the realms of interest. So in a sense Samuel Butler was right — "For purposes of mere reading, one book is as good as another"—for all books are avenues for the soul to go promenading, and they all have hinterlands in which the soul may take refuge. The moments and half moments when we do not exactly stop reading, but flash out during the eye pauses in reminiscences, conjectures, nuances of thought; and the minutes when we lay down the book, finger it lovingly as we examine the title with unseeing eyes, or fling it from us with a naughty word while the mind wanders on original excursions in quest of former vague thoughts long mislaid, or neglected ideas once glimpsed and beckoning but never salted, now tantalizingly evoked by a word said or left unsaid — these are the times when we really live; in the vernacular, *this is the life*. Unless we read in this way, the greater part of our spiritual history becomes nonexistent with the march of years. Reading will recall precisely those flashes of prescience or insight that once illumined our midnight, those priceless, evanescent bits of experience that vanish in a moment, those spiritual links that guarantee the continuity — or should I say immortality? — of the soul. Perhaps the pattern of human life remains drably the same because these shining threads that come to the hands of countless humble weavers slip unregarded to the floor.

5. And, finally, practice remembering. To read and make no effort to remember is the rankest folly and self-slaughter. J. B. Kerfoot tells how a friend asks him periodically, "John, how do you ever manage to remember all you read?" This question is common and frequently put to those whose business lies mainly among books. It implies that the memory is a cold-storage plant where all the books one has ever read are hung up by the heels. "George," replies the critic, "you eat three meals every day of the year. How do you manage to hold all you eat?" But George doesn't get it.

And now to return to the problem of reading in college. Sir Arthur Quiller-Couch, the inimitable "Q," says in *The Art of Reading*: "The first thing then to be noted about the reading of English . . . is that for Englishmen it has been made, by Act of Parliament, compulsory. The next thing to be noted is that in our schools and colleges and universities it has been made, by statute or in practice, all but impossible."

I have elsewhere had occasion to "view with alarm" the same dangerous approach to illiteracy in American colleges, and a nearly related phenomenon, the excessive requirement of papers in many college courses, a form of composition engendering a kind of unimaginative jargon, full of wise saws and modern instances, signifying nothing. Bad reading and bad writing are mutually cause and effect, but it is pretty generally agreed that reform in reading is strategically the place to begin.

A project in General Reading was begun in Hamline University in the fall of 1921 and in seven years has done a good deal to foster a healthy undergraduate interest in real books, as well as to spread the gospel of creative reading.

Generally speaking, in spite of some cynicism, the results are altogether hopeful. Students are evincing a steadily increasing interest in matching their reading powers with members of the faculty. In fact, much of the practical objection to the discussion plan comes from members of the faculty who feel that they cannot afford the time to prepare for what sometimes proves no tame academic exercise, but something of a battle. In our discussions we all realize better that the great books are democratic; they belong to all. An instructor in chemistry comes over from his laboratory to talk about Plato's *Republic* and find joy in the change; a professor of mathematics, who loves William DeMorgan, gets far away from functions and differentials with Joseph Vance; a classics scholar reveals to a somewhat astonished student that he is not unaware of Darwin; or a beloved professor of biology converses with intelligence and feeling on Huneker's *Overtones*. Great books are democratic and this reading is "general"; herein lies much of the virtue and charm of the business.

But it must not be supposed that slovenly reading need be winked at. On the contrary, this is an excellent time to call a bluff — good naturedly; or, if the bluffer persists in his bluffihood, with a touch of acid. The young bluffer ecclesiasticus, who imagines that because he is a semiprofessional pastor in the suburbs he need not give *Pilgrim's Progress* more than a patronizing once-over, gets a jolt from a history instructor, who, he has grave reason to suspect, is tainted with skepticism. And maybe he gets it in time. Another who cheerfully offers a jejune version of *Gulliver's Travels* which he acquired years before in an illustrated and expurgated edition, may discover in fifteen minutes more things he does not know about this great book than he had suspected he does not know about the whole eighteenth century. He will volunteer that the story is allegorical and will feel that he has said something. He will announce that Swift was a pessimist, amend that to cynic, and then perhaps find with chagrin that his notion of a cynic is about as nearly correct, though not nearly so definite, as that of the East Sider who told teacher, "A cyn-ic is what you wash dishes in."

Talking unguardedly about Shakespeare or Balzac or Walt Whitman is a certain way to bring out the most bizarre notions of what constitutes morality and immorality in literature. A girl whom Freud would have delighted to diagnose thought Whitman "terrible." She had read over and over certain well-advertised naughty poems and had merely skimmed "When Lilacs Last in the Door-Yard Bloomed" and "Pioneers, O Pioneers." When she added that Chaucer was "just plain nasty" and capped the climax by pronouncing Poe "too realistic," there seemed nothing to say to her that would have been polite or intelligible. This young woman was not graduated. Had she done well in the reading discussions she might have gained enough honor points to slip by; but then, if she had learned as a sophomore how to read, she would have been in no distress for honor points.

I have not yet mentioned one of the major virtues of these discussions between students and faculty. They offer unique opportunities to get acquainted. One may learn more of the mental quality of a student in an hour like this than he might discover in a whole year of formal classroom contacts. But the illumination one gets on students who come as complete strangers — and even in small colleges today no instructor is likely to know more than half the juniors and seniors — almost always proves of mutual interest and delight. Each instructor thus comes to know with some intimacy five or six ultimate alumni whom he would never otherwise have had even a bowing acquaintance with.

One final remark. This reading project is supplying in its

limited sphere one vital cultural deficiency of our age — in fact, a deficiency of every "modern" age. It is forging a link with the past, proving a conservator for these individuals of many fine things that have previously been dismissed as insignificant to the twentieth century. Plato and Aeschylus, *Piers Plowman* and More's *Utopia,* Lucretius, Epictetus and Lao-tze's *Tao Tê Ching* were read by none of the students six years ago; now a few, a growing few, are finding a lasting joy in them. The list of one hundred books was made without any thought of definite chronological distribution, but I find that thirty-seven, or slightly more than one third, were written before 1800 and sixty-three after 1800. I have charted the total reading of the current juniors and seniors and have been surprised to observe that almost exactly one third of the books read are the ancients. Perhaps that is not the full proportion that the ancients deserve, but the fault may be laid to the list; we have been too timid in our advocacy of indubitable classics. Apparently the students have no unalterable antipathy to a book more than a hundred years old.

I do not know whether people can ever succeed in both reading and riding at the same time. An ancient sophist proved there could be no motion, for a thing must be either where it is or where it is not; and since it is equally absurd to think of a thing moving where it is and where it is not, it must always remain stationary. He lived before the gas age. Now he might have observed that a nation of riders, always going somewhere else, are *never* where they are, but always where they are not. For we live in our minds, or nowhere; and our minds are always somewhere else. Reading requires a harbor anchorage. I think after all I shall defer a little longer joining that vast army of uneasy spirits invoked by the genius of Detroit and engaged in living where they are not.

The old trivium of the R's, Reading and 'Riting and 'Rithmetic, has given way to the new trivium, Reeling and Riding and Picture Shows. A static quality was inherent in the three R's, while movement is all in the new prescription. It is likely that every age will continue to try to square the circle, to eat its cake and have it, too, and to discover the secret of perpetual motion. Ours has come near to the last; so near that it would be expecting miracle on miracle to hope that it can go on riding and continue to read.

There is a practical necessity for creative reading. Except by learning to swim we cannot hope to survive much longer the ever-swelling rivers of printers' ink.

Valentine

DEDICATED *to the photographs of Thomas and Jane Welsh Carlyle, hanging in our home, near the fireplace.*

Said Tom to Jeannie,
  "Ma bonnie queanie,
    Dodge out and fetch the candles;
    For I thocht of a gude word
    That sings like a wude bird.
    I must shoot him while he dandles."

Said Jane to Tom,
  "Ma monnie Tom,
    Get up yoursel', you hatchet,
    For I ha' a bad one
    Can top any mad one,
    And you are like to catch it."

Then said Thomas to Jane,
  "I'd no mak' ye vain,
    But you're like a thustle in a field of heather."
    And Jane came back with a burry crack:
  "Ah Tom, we're two stickers together."

At His Beddes Heed Twenty Bookes

LAST *month, when honored by an invitation to speak on this occa-*
sion, remembering how I had a decade ago said the best thing I
knew, I cast furiously about in my mind for a topic. I set down thir-
teen, and they all seemed good; but they were all, for some reason,
invalid. So I did what I have learned to be a smart thing: I consulted
some students, members of the class who were to be the targets. As
a matter of fact, I considered making the subject of this talk "What
I have learned from students"; and I rather wish I had stuck to that
plan.

These are some of the good hints I received:

Don't talk about everything. Say something about something.

Better not indulge in a great deal of reminiscence.

Don't try to talk about the atomic bomb; we've heard about that
baby.

Don't tell us what a mess the world is in; that topic has been
worried sufficiently.

And as a corollary to that last one, Don't tell us that we can make
a "brave new world." Even God Almighty didn't create the universe
out of nothing; He had to have Chaos, and all we have is the debris
you have left from your world.

And so, like good teachers, they set me a hard task: to keep out
of the smooth, well-worn grooves, and to say something about some-
thing that I knew something about.

ANATOLE FRANCE wrote down often his view that
no man talks about anything but himself. Said he:
"Gentlemen, I am going to talk about myself on the
subject of Shakespeare, or Racine, or Pascal, or Goethe —
subjects that offer me a beautiful opportunity."

In a similar vein, since a good part of my life has been
spent in trying to become acquainted with some of the vast
literary heritage of our race, I want to talk to you about
Faith on the topic of "My Best Books."

NOTE. Cap and Gown Day Address at Hamline University, April 1947.

Chaucer's Clerk of Oxford

> *was levere have at his beddes heed*
> *Twenty bookes clad in blak or reed*
> *Of Aristotle and his philosophië*
> *Than robes riche, or fithele or gay sautrië.*

Since my early teaching days my chief indoor sport has been making up lists of good books and scheming to get other people to read them. I discovered in an old scrapbook that the *Oracle* published in 1917 an article by me, which I assure you the editor had solicited, called "Fifty Loaded Books." Since then I have twice assisted in choosing lists of great books in the hope of furthering the cause of education. They were not strictly my books: of some of them I could pretend to but little firsthand knowledge. They were partly hearsay, but good hearsay. However, I want to name the twenty books that have been at my bed's head — and side — and from which I have largely drawn whatever faith is in me.

I shall not give summaries or critiques of all of them. I shall merely name them, and say something about a few that I cannot endure being silent about.

There are some surprising omissions. "Of Aristotle and his philosophie" I shall have nothing to say, not because he is not to me a great and revered name, but because he has not been one of my constant inspirations. On the other hand Wood's *Heavenly Discourses*, by no standard a "great book," has given me a peculiar satisfaction over many years, as have Hardy's novels and poems, though I have no time to dwell on either Wood or Hardy.

1. The Bible needs no explanation, no apology in standing first. But not the whole of the motley compilation which we call *the* Bible. The books I name will not stretch the covers of a good-sized octavo volume: Genesis, Job, Psalms, Tobit, Isaiah, Jeremiah, Amos, the Four Gospels, the Acts,

the Epistle of James, and certain of Paul's epistles, especially Corinthians, Thessalonians, and Hebrews.

2. Confucius, *Four Books* (Analects, The Mean, The Higher Learning, Mencius).

3. Lao-tze, *Tao Tê Ching*.

4. Epictetus, *Discourses*.

5. Plato, *Socratic Dialogues*.

6. Chaucer, *Troilus and Criseyde*.

7. Shakespeare, six or eight plays (*Hamlet, Merchant of Venice, Lear, Tempest, Macbeth, Henry IV, Henry V, Othello*).

8. Milton, sonnets, *Lycidas, Areopagitica, Paradise Lost,* and *Samson Agonistes*.

9. Montaigne, *Essais*.

10. Wood, C. E. S., *Heavenly Discourses*.

11. Swift, *Gulliver's Travels, Tale of a Tub*, and *Letter to a Young Clergyman*.

12. Boswell, *Life of Samuel Johnson*.

13. Carlyle, *Sartor Resartus*.

14. Lincoln, speeches and letters.

15. Melville, *Moby Dick*.

16. Dostoevski, *The Brothers Karamazov*.

17. Marx and Engels, *The Communist Manifesto*.

18. Whitman, *Leaves of Grass*.

19. Hardy, novels and poems.

20. Thoreau, *A Week on the Concord and Merrimac Rivers*, and essays including "Walking," and "The Duty of Civil Disobedience."

I am tempted to name another twenty or fifty without which I should be crippled; but without these twenty I should not *be*. Out of these largely have come my faith. Since faith is needed today as at few times in human history, it is not an unworthy effort to set down the specific articles of faith that have entered into one individual specimen of the genus *homo*; it may be indeed that our species

(I hesitate to say *sapiens*) will not remain much longer on the earth. The next species may prove more sapient, but I doubt that it will write better books.

The first article of faith is faith in the books themselves. No number of books about these books, or books about books about these books, or lectures about them can take the place of the books themselves. And these books are not to be read *for themselves*. Don't read the Bible for the Bible's sake, or even for God's sake. Read it for your own sake and the sake of the world in which you live.

It may seem completely otiose to urge you to read the Bible. The Bible is so important a library of books that we should not be content with one copy, one translation, one version. I still consult most frequently the India paper King James edition which my mother gave me when I went away from home for the first time. But I have many others at "my beddes heed."

They are the English revision and the American revision of the late nineteenth century, Moulton's *Modern Readers' Bible*, which was an innovator in the idea of applying modern editorial technique in arrangement and organization, the New Standard Revision, and the Basic English version of the New Testament. Besides I have Wyclif's Job and the New Testament (fourteenth century), and the West Saxon Psalms and Gospels (tenth or eleventh century). Then a great source of pleasure and enlightenment has been the German Bible, based on Luther, and the French New Testament after the version of Ostervald. I am, unfortunately, not able to read the Greek original, but I have found light on many an obscure passage thrown by the rational clarity of the French. The most startling example is found in Acts 17:23. I had always thought Paul singularly lacking in diplomacy in the report that he said to the Athenians, "Whom ye ignorantly worship, him declare I unto you." The French translator (whether closer to the Greek or not I do not know, nor am I much concerned) has this: "The one whom you honor without knowing him, I make known to you now." This is brilliant tact and, I am eager to believe, an appealing approach to Athenians by a Roman citizen who was intelligent enough to recognize how much Rome owed to Greece.

The Sermon on the Mount is sufficient in itself to place the New Testament at the pinnacle of wisdom literature. The Christian church and Christian tradition has not yet absorbed these seven octavo pages into its living belief. Consider one example only: "Take care not to do your good works before men, to be seen by them; or you will have no reward from your Father in heaven. When then you give money to the poor, do not make a noise about it, as the false-hearted men do in the Synagogues and in the streets, so that they may have glory from men. But when you give money, let not your right hand see what your left hand does. . . ."

The blare of charities and philanthropies is raucous in the ears of God. We cannot separate from this faith the skepticism of Jesus concerning the prayers that are said in public places. He had more faith in those that came from private rooms and were not expressed in definitive words. How different might be our living of the wisdom of Jesus if we cut our New Testament down to those seven pages and perhaps another fifty!

From Confucius the great article of faith is one rooted in humanity. A grounding in Confucius will strengthen the faith in the dignity of man. And to my way of thinking the so-called negative golden rule is a valuable adjunct to that of Jesus. Confucius had a realistic conception of what is possible for men; he realized the strength of the negative. "Do not to another what you would not have him do to you." This is in easy reach. I can vividly call to mind at a particular moment something I devoutly hope a person with whom I have contact will not do to me. If I have firmly fixed in consciousness the negative rule of Confucius, then that is the very thing I will not do to him. There is no excuse for me if I forget it, and there is little likelihood that I shall. On the other hand, "*Whatsoever* ye would that men should do to you, do ye even so to them" has not such a sharp focus. I want so many things from other people. How can I be blamed if I do not have them all in mind at a particular moment and so absent-mindedly fail to carry out toward another one of the things I hope he will do for me. And furthermore, can I be blamed if the one thing I forget happens to be the very thing I *could* do at the moment?

For the student especially, Confucius has a burning article of faith: "If a man loves kindness, but does not love study, his short-coming will be ignorance." And ignorance in one who could be knowing (not to say wise) is a sin of the first order. What a revolution in the processes of education if dilatory students could become convicted of sin!

Epictetus is said to have been a Phrygian, the slave of a profligate freedman of the time of Nero. It was smart in the first century A.D. to own an educated slave — an artist, a musician, or, best of all, a philosopher. Through manumission or otherwise, Epictetus obtained his freedom from Epaphroditus and set up a Stoic school at Nicopolis. Here he taught, but wrote no more than did Confucius or Socrates. His pupil Arrian took down many of his sayings, and put them forth in eight books, four of which are extant under the name of *Discourses* or the *Enchiridion*.

The classic translation is by George Long, who also made a good translation of that other popular Stoic philosopher, the Emperor Marcus Aurelius. To me the slave spoke more powerfully than the emperor. Between the ages of eighteen and twenty-five I spent a lot of time in his company. Perhaps too much, I later thought. But at that time I got what I needed — a hard Stoic shell which protected my ego from many a bruise. Epictetus harps much on one string: certain things are in our power; the wise man pays no attention to what is not in his power. Permit me to quote a bit from the chapter, "That we ought not to be angry with the errors (faults) of others": "Do not admire your clothes, and then you will not be angry with the thief. Consider this matter thus: you have fine clothes; your neighbor has not; you have a window; you wish to air the clothes. The thief does not know wherein man's good consists, but he thinks that it consists in having fine clothes, the very thing which you also think. Must he not then come and take them away? When you show a cake to greedy persons, and swallow it all yourself, do you expect them not to snatch it from you? Do not provoke them; do not have a window; do not air your clothes . . . For a man only loses that which he has. I have lost my garment. The reason is that you had a garment. I have a pain in my head. Have you any pain in your horns? . . . Do not say, Alas, I have pain in the ear. Do not say alas. And I do not say that you are not allowed to groan, but do not groan inwardly."

The time came when I began to think this was not the final wisdom; although Carlyle about the same period in my life came to the aid of Epictetus with his great neo-romantic, neo-Stoic principle in *Sartor Resartus*, "The fraction of life is not so much increased by increasing the numerator as by decreasing the denominator . . ." The oft-repeated article of faith of this nineteenth century Stoic was: Seek not happiness; seek blessedness! "What if thou wert born and predestined not to be happy, but to be unhappy!" No one can claim that Carlyle did his groaning *inwardly*. He told the world. And why not? A man with his power of language shouldn't have to rot with all his language in him. His repudiation of happiness, even of practical usefulness as an end, and his ringing faith in Natural Supernaturalism, in the universe as the living Garment of God, or God as the Soul of the Universe, was a good faith in 1833 and it remains a good faith in 1947.

Milton, except the sweet melodies of "L'Allegro," "Il Penseroso" and "Comus," and the thunderous oratory of the first two books of *Paradise Lost,* came late into my life. But he has set up a chain reaction which I cannot do justice to in a paragraph. Milton the artist, like Dostoevski, has given me a better understanding of the fourth dimension than I have been able to learn from Einstein and a complete sense of participation in a multiple ordinal world. Others may have presented better arguments for the freedom of the will (I do not know who they are), but no one has expressed so passionately the human need for it nor has given such capacity to *believe* in it. *Areopagitica* is the supreme classic on freedom of speech and of the press, to be sure, but that is not all it is. One passage in it, almost a casual passage, explodes that perennial but particularly modern fallacy of the elementalism which permits us to compartmentalize the various aspects of this human life:

"What should he do? Fain he would have the name to be religious, fain he would bear up with his neighbors in that. What does he therefore, but resolves to give over toiling, and to find himself out some factor or agent . . . He entertains his religion, gives him gifts, feasts him, lodges him; his religion comes home at night, prays, is liberally supped, and sumptuously laid to sleep; rises, is saluted, and after the malmsey his religion walks abroad at eight and leaves his kind entertainer in the shop, trading all day without his religion."

After reading that how can I ever again put my religion, my business, my politics, and my recreations into different stalls and expect them never to rub noses?

Knowing John Milton induces a faith in the unity of the human spirit.

I doubt if anyone can be said to have read *Gulliver's Travels* who has not read it three times — once as a child, once as a youth in high school or college, and then as a mature man or woman. The first time, he reads a good yarn; the second time, he comes to a shaking-of-the-head acquaintance with a terrible man, a cynic and pessimist, a hater of mankind. On the third reading, the mature reader by the grace of God gets a formal introduction to the only man of the early eighteenth century who had the heart to feel the plight of the Irish bog-trotter, and the man who more than any other man of his time, hated hypocrisy and at the same time knew how to scotch it.

The Mosaic commandment, "Thou shalt not bear false witness against thy neighbor," has always left a loophole by its legal language for lying and especially cheating. The "New Decalogue" of Arthur Hugh Clough introduces these revisions: "Thou shalt not steal; an empty feat when 'tis as lucrative to cheat"; "Bear not false witness; let the lie have time on its own wings to fly." The mission of most of the world's great satirists has been to hold the liar and the hypocrite up to scorn. Rabelais, Erasmus, Cervantes, Mark Twain, even Fielding gives the hypocrite something of a sporting chance, but when Swift pursues his quarry I can almost pity the cowering wretch. Yet not quite, for Swift gives us a strong faith that God hates a lie. It is not enough to love the truth; we must implement that love by hating a lie.

Montaigne I love especially for two reasons: his complete intellectual honesty and his beautiful capacity for friendship. "A liar," he wrote, "must be brave toward God and a coward toward men." Writing of his friend Stephen La Boetie, he said, "If anyone would importune me to give a reason why I love him, I feel it could no otherwise be expressed than by giving answer 'Because it was he; because it was I.'"

America has its place in my twenty with Lincoln, Melville, Thoreau, and Whitman. If we could only claim their essence for a definition of democracy, what a happy heritage for a people! It is not easy — nor necessary — to reconcile on a superficial level the sage of Walden and the sage of Sangamon, Springfield, Washington, and the world. But Thoreau on "The Duty of Civil Disobedience" to a bad government is not far from the war president whose duty it was to uphold the constituted government wherein it was *just*, but whose greater duty it was to render it just. "If I have unjustly wrested a plank from a drowning man," says Thoreau, "I must restore it to him though I drown myself. . . . But he that would save his life in such a case, shall lose it. This people must cease to hold slaves, and to make war on Mexico, though it cost them their existence as a people."

A little later Lincoln was to make his great speech on "a house divided against itself," and still a little later was to give his life a vicarious sacrifice for the "nation divided against itself," as truly as his acknowledged Master who climbed the Hill of Golgotha.

Abraham Lincoln is not to be found in the more than three thousand books that have been written about him. He is to be found in his own letters and speeches and telegrams: "With malice toward none, with charity for all . . ." "That we here highly resolve . . . that this nation, under God, shall have a new birth of freedom, and that government of the people, by the people, for the people, shall not perish from the earth." "When any church will inscribe over its altar . . . the Savior's condensed statement of the substance of both Law and Gospel, 'Thou shalt love the Lord Thy God with all thy heart and with all thy mind, and thy neighbor as thyself' that church will I join with all my heart and with all my soul." "I am not much of a judge of religion, but in my opinion, the religion that sets men to rebel and fight against their government because, as they think, that government does not sufficiently help some men to eat their bread in the sweat of other men's faces, is not the sort of religion upon which people can get to heaven."

That this man of Olympian calm and peace above the strife, this man of unbroken patience, this man of near Christ-like magnitude should have had also that most endearing human capstone of humor in a supreme quality and measure seems a gift to posterity more than it deserves.

If one wishes to experience a full-bodied, full-blooded, full-spirited religion, capable of bulldozing his soul out of the slough of materialism, he must believe in the Second Inaugural Address.

There may be some who will be shocked at finding the *Communist Manifesto* among my bedside books. Or, if not surprised, they may feel it a breach of decorum to range Marx along with these other books of faith. But I believe there will be no sense of impropriety among those who have read these epochal forty pages. If we are to live in one world, we must live in a world integrated by many articles of faith that on a certain level will at first appear inconsistent.

Personally, I find it possible, nay, imperative, to believe in certain truths enunciated one hundred years ago by Karl Marx and Friedrich Engels, and those I live by — try to live by — in the Sermon on the Mount. And one of my deepest regrets is the historic anomaly that prevented Thomas Carlyle and Abraham Lincoln and Karl Marx from knowing each other and forming incidences which might have prevented the false oppositions into which their disciples have forced them. *Past and Present* and the Emancipation Proclamation contain the same kind of social dynamite that is found in the *Communist Manifesto,* and is corollary to that of the original TNT in the New Testament. For example: "The bourgeoisie, wherever it has got the upper hand, has put an end to all feudal, patriarchal, idyllic relations. It has . . . left no other nexus between man and man than naked self-interest, than callous 'cash payment.' It has drowned the most heavenly ecstacies of religious fervor, of chivalrous enthusiasm, in the icy water of egotistical calculation. It has resolved personal worth into exchange value, and in place of the numberless indefeasible chartered freedoms, has set up that single, unconscionable freedom—Free Trade. In one word, for exploitation, veiled by religious and political illusions, it has substituted naked, shameless, direct, brutal exploitation."

It will be the hard but not impossible task of the class of 1947, 1948, 1949, 1950, and the classes of the next generation to find a way to join effectively these complementary articles of faith. They may be forged only "as by fire," and the forging process must take place in the individual minds.

Some say the World will end in fire,
Some say in ice.
From what I've tasted of desire
I hold with those who favor fire.
But if it had to perish twice,
I think I know enough of hate
To say that for destruction ice
Is also great,
And would suffice.

Like Robert Frost, but with a difference, I favor fire, the fire of the forge. But I fear Ice—the ice of mutual distrust, of ignorance, of hatred. Let us put our trust in the forge of faith, excluding no seer of truth, and beginning where we are, by understanding all those who have seen life however imperfectly, but have seen it truly, passionately, and in love. Let us take up wholeheartedly our inescapable burden of providing the forge of faith.

Killing Time

THE writer is unfortunately not a sociologist; he does not have the information or the genius to deal with the sudden, obvious, spectacular suicides committed with revolver, steel, water, gas, or Prussic acid. Neither is he a moralist, fitted to speak with authority upon the slower methods of poisoning, such as alcohol, tobacco, coffee, tea, and the like. Nor yet is he an economist, brevetted to speak gravely of the habit of reckless living. All these methods of killing one's physical self quickly are out of the present scope. They are charted so boldly by statisticians and deplored so eloquently by public oracles that it may be inferred that we are on our guard against them.

And they do not constitute real suicide.

To commit suicide is to kill one's self, and one's self cannot be killed in an instant any more than one's self can be born in an instant. To admit, as common custom does, that a self may develop through bud and blossom to fruit, only to be annihilated by a single physical act, a drink or a thrust or an explosion, is the limit of illogic. Even if we hold what is not unlikely, that physical death ends all for some people who have not taken the trouble to develop a soul, these people would still have achieved a kind of undesirable immortality in the influences they have set working during their lives, a web which would in a sense keep alive their selves to the end of the cosmic period in which they were cast. Life, personal salvation involving individual development in eternity, may not be for all; but immortality in the sense of Maeterlinck, survival in the minds of per-

NOTE. An early version appeared in the *Midwest Quarterly*, June 1918.

sons still living or in active forces, none can escape. That is, none save those who have learned how to kill themselves through the long years in the slow and deadly manner which I have to indicate.

To kill time is to commit suicide in the surest, deadliest manner possible.

In that splendid work of gloomy genius, Dostoevski's *The House of the Dead,* the Siberian exiles speak of their crimes in the most matter-of-fact, even light-hearted manner. What we call crime has become for them normal and moral in a sense. It does not occur to the confirmed criminals even to boast of their crimes, as the occasional and hysterical wrongdoer frequently boasts. Just so have we come to speak of the most universal and effective method of taking human life in this indulgent, bantering way as "killing time." Intellectual workers even make virtue of their crimes and justify certain vicious methods of dulling and stupefying the mind with the whitewashing title of "recreation."

Foremost among the sleek villains whom we enlist as accomplices in this conscienceless self-slaughter is Reading to Pass the Time. He is invited early for the children, and from the moment they learn to read, life is one long sad decline. Reading seems to be regarded by many parents as a harmless amusement, in the pursuit of which, provided the reading matter be not intrinsically harmful — that is, improper — a boy or girl can get into no mischief. This assumption is based upon a truth, for getting into mischief implies an active self, whereas pastime reading is the negation of self. It arrests development for at least the actual duration of the reading, usually for longer; it cuts out of life an hour, two hours, a half day — and gives no return. At least, that is the ideal of the pastime reading which is recommended to growing children as a sedative during digestion. The effect could not be more maleficent if the boy or girl took some soporific drug and instead of reading Alger, Rollo, interminable Boy Scout serials, Superman, "Terry and the Pirates," or any of the What Every Child Should Know brand of printed stuff, slept away the time.

In fact, the effect of a drug would not be nearly so bad; for not simply that hour or that half day is killed, but the *memory* of the time is permitted to die. Books which contain no facts nor situations nor lines to remember are meant to be forgotten and forgotten they are. They have served their purpose; they have passed some time. They have done more; they have attacked the memory.

Nothing so quickly dulls and deadens the powers of memory as paying no attention to the duty of remembering. The boy who reads a highly edifying and utterly bald story in the Sunday School *Weekly Visitor*, a vapid, conventional romance in *Golden Hours*, the puerile narratives of Rollo, a "comic" picture serial, or anything which, requiring the attention of the self for the moment, is immediately relegated to limbo, will find it just a little harder the next day to get his history lesson. His subliminal mind says to his self, "What you read yesterday didn't make any difference; nothing makes any difference; it is all pastime." And so after every indulgence the memory becomes more torpid, and before long William the Conqueror takes his place in the same Gehenna of twilight recollection as the last hero of characterless impeccability. Of course, the duty lies upon all of us to forget the negligible that comes to us in the ordinary course of the commonplace, and there will always be enough of the negligible coming in that way. But it is surely a crime to proceed in cold blood to give the child entertainment and keep him out of mischief by suggesting reading that offers his mind no assimilative pabulum and demands of every self-respecting mind chiefly to be forgotten. "For purposes of mere reading," says Samuel Butler, "one book is as good as another." This farcical bon mot is taken very seriously by many grownup persons and by some pedagogical systems as well—provided always the book is of a respectable mediocrity. It is the custom of these persons and these systems to decry the sensational, the penny dreadful, the blood and thunder. Whereas a moment's reflection should be enough to convince sensible people that it is better for a boy to read stories of wild or sensational grip than stories of no grip at all. Blood and thunder is better than drivel; Nick Carter is infinitely superior to the mild monotony of Rollo. Indeed, it is hardly too much to say that an immoral story remembered is better for the self than a moral one forgotten. For the self is impossible without memory to hold the consecutive moments together, and any force which destroys or impairs memory kills life.

The world is full of people who bemoan a poor memory and envy a good one. In nearly every case either they sinned or their parents and teachers before them, for all healthy children have good memories. There can be little doubt of this statement. The brain in normal life varies only slightly in sensitiveness to impression. Between the most and the least sensitive there is probably, to be sure, a wide gulf, but the average retentiveness of childhood is very high. Since nearly every adult who suffers from faulty memory is perfectly sure that as a child he remembered easily, it seems almost certain that the evil slyly enters somewhere in the education, usually before the years of adolescence. The mother who reads one fairy tale after another, passing from sensation to sensation without comment or reflection, is marring the delicately sensitized plate of the brain cortex and teaching it to forget. It is small wonder that the child continues to kill his *self* as he grows up, for he has learned the art from those who love him best. Unless somewhere in the educational experience of the child he receives help in selecting and emphasizing certain of the myriad impressions that come to him daily without bringing with them any necessary reflection or any hint of meaning, he will, unless he fortunately stumbles upon some form of right self-education, soon be possessed of a brain traced with a million impressions, significant and insignificant together, which gradually have the effect of scarring the sensitive surface and rendering permanent memory increasingly hard.

On second thought it seems evident that the charge of suicide should give way to one of murder.

For "hammock fiction," on the other hand, there is suppositionally at least some justification. We are told that the tired businessman and the jaded housewife must have books of that kind. Certainly, they honestly believe they must, and as long as there continues the insistent demand, commercial gentlemen who write romances will do well in their generation to manufacture the supply. It was said that the war of 1914-1918 pushed the art of flying so rapidly that airplanes four months old became antiquated. World War II has antiquated everything but jet robot planes and products of atomic fission. Observers of ephemeral literature will not be surprised, for since the origin of the best seller, fictions more than four months old have come to be regarded as antiques by the people who buy new novels. A busy devotee who once gets behind the book of the moment placidly lets it go on, while he turns to catch the book of the next moment on the wing.

In truth, there would be something splendid about this voracity for living in the present, if the tired businessman aimed at remembering and the commercial gentlemen who write aimed at the rememberable — conditions contrary to fact. The irony of the situation lies here: fiction, while it rests the mind in providing a change of activity, does not rest it so much as history or popular metaphysics or poetry would by stinging the mind of the tired businessman into impersonal reflection, and fiction is more wearing physically on him than real books would be.

The last fact is easily demonstrable to any one who will give it the slightest examination. Look into the eyes of one reading a light novel. They fairly race back and forth over the lines — one, two, three, jump, and back to the next line; one, two, three, and back; one, two, three, and back. There is nothing to cause the mind to parley and the eyes keep up their short, hysterical dashes. That is the reason why at the end of an hour's steady reading of an exciting romance one's eyes ache and burn and demand a rest before setting out on the chase again. Now turn to another reader, engaged upon a book of content, like Bergson's *Laughter* or William James's *Will to Believe* or Toynbee's *A Study of History* or a poem in the *Viking Book of Poetry* or an anthology by Untermeyer or Rodman. The eyes merely march across the page in sober delight, pausing frequently for the mind to catch up, to permit the memory to impress a fact, or to question a principle, or to enjoy the savor of an image or symbol. The physical wear and tear of such books is not half that of hammock fiction, and moreover the mental exertion is, to practical people whose days are taken up with concrete detail, more restful than morphine. I am quite sure that human lives would be richer and more people would work out souls with a chance of surviving physical death if all the hammock fiction and pastime reading, together with nine tenths of the newspaper were providentially destroyed. The art of printing cannot be seriously discredited even by excessive laudation; it was midwife to the modern mind and modern culture. This should not blind us, however, to the danger that a surfeit of printed words is likely to prove the most vicious form of race suicide.

Of most of the numerous little kill-times, I say nothing. Suppose that a savior of traveling men should give them a substitute for solitaire when they are stranded away from home in a cheerless country hotel. Or suppose that the good star of elderly ladies should discover to them a remedy for

70

the ennui of bridge, for it is well recognized that the ennui of the game itself is only a trifle less severe than the ennui of being deprived of it. Or suppose that the time squandered in idle mooning should be added to our completely conscious lives.

Nor do I at this writing arraign Big Talk, who is the arch-murderer; he is too important a criminal to deal with adequately or with propriety in a paper on suicide. No commutal of sentence can make his offense manslaughter or even murder in the second degee. It is stark, naked murder, following by pillage and rapine. Having killed an hour of our time, which is our life, the skillful public speaker, political, aesthetic, social, religious, robs us of our reason and commits assault and battery on our judgment. We do not jail him because in our age punishment like gravitation is in inverse proportion to the square of the offense.

Passing these by, we come to a close rival of Pastime Reading, the second villain of the play, Small Talk. Small Talk is one of the most effective methods of suicide. Perhaps there is much to be said in the defense of the inanities of polite discourse, with whose devious ways we are all more or less familiar. At least, it is not of them I am thinking, not of the meaningless chatter of the stand-up reception, not even of gossip in its various malodorous degrees, for it has been the subject of animadversion enough. What I have in mind is more intellectually respectable and vicious. It is more commonly prevalent among intellectuals, perhaps commonest of all in college circles; it goes with the pride of intellect. I mean the talk between two people or in small groups which takes form as myriads of little futile rills of inconclusive argument, starting from unexamined premises, and ending exactly where it began because each party to the talk sets his feet and sinks deeper in the rut of his preconceptions and prejudices. He does not convince the others, but he strengthens himself in his formulated — that is,

71

dead — opinions. After every chaotic debate in which the contestants do not take the pains to reduce and sift the argument, but merely content themselves with categoric, dogmatic statements (the true cat and dog method), each one is a deader man. He has deepened his grave and thrust himself farther into it. By positive committal to a doubtful view he has made it more difficult to reach a new conclusion. By saying a thing with assurance which in the beginning he only half believed, he is forced in point of honor — that is, pride of intellectual infallibility — to adopt it thereafter and defend it with martyr zeal. He is less capable of moving freely in the current of living thought and of interpreting the flow of his past history.

Talk with no sincere desire to learn is false; it is out of harmony with the *élan vital*; life is to it still medieval, syllogistic, static. It may even be doubted whether teachers and prophets can deliver any message worth while as long as they remain convinced that they have reached the last word on their subject. Sincere learners are the only genuine teachers, and the talk proceeding from settled convictions is usually as dead as the Sahara desert.

A memory stored with the best moments of the past is proof against ennui and is entirely independent of the ordinary machinery for killing the present. Moreover, it is the only native source of sure strength against temptation in the present. The man who remembers the high moments in his life when tempted to a mean or vile action, who lives over the day of his best love, his most splendid sacrifice, his deepest joy or darkest sorrow, the birth of his soul, the exact details in all their delicate particularities of his Golgotha and his Calvary — the man who *can* remember these, whose memory has not become a spiritual palimpsest requiring the erasure of the subtle past to make room for the blatant present, is in a mood for strenuous things, not for the idle, vain, capricious, low.

Yet the ironical thing is that our leisure time is devoted to forgetting, that is, to the neglect of these connecting links that bind the *disjecta membra* of our experience into a unified life. How many men and women have a vivid sense of their past spiritual history? I do not mean facts and dates, though even these are quick to escape in the turmoil of the struggle for existence. What man of thirty remembers how and what he thought at twenty? how a look or a letter affected him? just how a poem or a play or a song gave a new bent to his conduct? Even those who possess their past most completely are conscious of many a breach. One of our commonest experiences is a shiver and start as at sight of a ghost when a freak of association drags out of the lumber room of the memory some great, important epoch long neglected. Memory says to us, "You and that silly, poetic boy of fifteen years ago are the same"; but it is a mere "brute fact" to us. We accept it as we do the daily miracles, shrug our shoulders, and say that it is "funny." As for being able to trace a line of descent from that silly, poetic boy to the present solid, self-satisfied man, we are as helpless as Topsy.

This means that we are not the possessors of our whole lives. We have killed and buried much of our past. Some of it may be indeed better so. "Forgetting the things that are behind" can advantageously apply both to defeats and successes. But the things we cannot afford to lose — less disastrous would be the loss of the future — are the times of soul growth, the high resolves, the flashes of prescience that illumined our midnight. These constitute our surest evidence of a soul and the surest guarantee of immortality — and it is exactly these priceless bits of experience that vanish in a moment. If we do not recall and recall again these evanescent gleams, we rob our lives of their significance.

To "loaf and invite the soul" is the way to retain its spiritual history; yet the leisure hour in which alone these moments would have a chance to survive across the welter of life's activity we devote to pastime reading or talk. I cannot escape the conviction that we are face to face with tragedy. We truly and completely live only in our idle moments — and these we stifle, partly because we are afraid of ghosts but mainly because we live in an age of printed and spoken words. So the years are spent, in active and passive neglect of their finest fruitage, and as age succeeds age, the pattern of human life and thought remains dreadfully the same. Most of the shining threads that come to the hands of the weavers are thrown away, and few of them are ever found again.

FOR A SUMMER SUNDAY

On Sunday when the church-bells ring,
Go and find you a willow swing;
A willow swing that creaks and bows
Above a stream that seaward flows,
With a ceaseless monody our heart knows.

What matters the name of the river there?
Close your eyes and 'tis Afton or Ayr.
Close your eyes and hold them tight;
Throw wide the portals of soul for sight,
The colors of fancy your thought bedight.

Oh, go and find you a willow swing;
Sway and rock in your windy sling;
Change for gold your lead and tin,
Stop your ears to discord and din,
And welcome God's orchestration in.

China and the United States

This and the next essay, written after a year of teaching in China, seemed to demand revision in the light of the succeeding kaleidoscopic years. But the attempt involved root-and-branch historical treatment far beyond the author's purpose and capacity. Therefore, with the concurrence of several good critics, he has somewhat reluctantly allowed the local and temporal allusions to stand as of 1925, trusting the reader of 1948 to find something still contemporary.

There was a temptation to slip in here and there allusions to occurrences since 1925; but the whole warp would have changed; the aim would have grown more complicated and pretentious, and the results would have become even less effective than they are without meddling.

FOR many reasons the world today is keeping an interested eye on China. A "cycle of Cathay," as Tennyson excusably did not know, is a period of sixty years, symbolized by the face of the clock. Since 1911 then, barely a quarter of a cycle has elapsed. However, almost any year of the fifteen offers a better observation of dramatic forces than may be found in a decade of postbellum Europe.

These United States have special and unusual reasons for an ardent concern in the current history and the probable goal of the great trans-Pacific republic. First of all, we have the interest of a benefactor, for despite mistakes and fallings from grace, America deserves the esteem that she has won from the Chinese as their traditional friend. The college founded by a remitted portion of the American Boxer Indemnity at beautiful Tsing Hua Yuan, in whose service I have just spent a year of varied charm, is a solid monument to enlightened American statesmanship and to the gratitude

NOTE. First published in the *American Review*, March-April 1926.

of a people who in return for kindness know how to keep faith.

When the Chinese people invited the Manchu to retire, they did not, like the Japanese on the eve of their modernization, model their new state after Britain or Germany; they looked with admiration at America and modeled their government after ours. Indeed they too nearly *adopted* it without the changes proper to their different needs. They also sought counsel of American experts and technicians in many fields.

From another point of view America has an interest in China because these two republics, vis-à-vis on opposite sides of the Pacific basin, hold in their hands their own mutual welfare and the destiny of the earth's future. Aside from sentimental and traditional reasons, self-interest and an enlightened view of world affairs require that America and China understand each other.

China has been accredited, whether properly or improperly, with many inventions and advances upon civilization. Printing and gunpowder, the modern media of brain-right and fist-right, are pretty certainly the offspring of Chinese genius, though it is but just to remember that the intent behind the invention of explosives was nothing murderous. That intent was altogether festive. Weddings and birthdays were in the minds of its progenitors; not seige guns and depth bombs.

Not so generally remarked, though no less indubitable, is the fact that China gave the world its first practical experiments in state socialism. The first of these experiments, according to Chancellor Tsai of the National University in Peking, was in the fifth century B.C. though the most famous of all occurred much later. Under the Sungs, in the eleventh century A.D., an enlightened minister named Wang An-shih, aiming at the ideal of abolishing poverty and the idle rich, declared: "The state should take the entire management of commerce, industry and agriculture into its own hands, with the view of succoring the working classes, and preventing their being ground to the dust by the rich." He specifically advocated the following measures: an empire-wide system of marketing with the state acting as middleman; remeasurement of the land and a new levy of taxes in proportion to the fertility of the soil; and an educational reform in the direction of practical or vocational subjects. The first only is of immediate interest to my theme, though the others are remarkable enough. Wang An-shih carried everything before him for a time, but in his old age had the misfortune and pain to see the failure of his enlightened plans. His failure was due not merely to the intrenched ignorance of both common folk and literati, but to a succession of natural calamities such as floods and consequent pestilences and famines which, though they have been China's immemorial sorrow, were used by his enemies as proof that his theories were essentially impious and displeasing to the gods.

This well-nigh forgotten incident is worthy of recall at the present when the industrial future of China is a matter of paramount concern.

Today China is awake; not, as is so often sentimentally said, after a sleep of centuries, but after only a little more than a hundred years of comatose dotage. There is no truth in the picture of a stationary or degenerate nation from the time of Confucius to the present. Greece was great for only two centuries; China has shown repeated bursts of creative energy and over a total of many more epochs of advance than any other historic people.

In the center of the renowned Chou dynasty, 1122-255 B.C., stand Lao-tze and K'ung-tze (Confucius) and Moh-tze, a triumvirate not far below the wise men of Greece. The streams of influence started by these sages are still flowing. After the reaction of the great and infamous Ch'in and the quiet days of Han came a remarkable outburst of artistic creation which lasted throughout the period of the Tangs, 618-906 A.D. During these stretches of dark, barbarous, anarchic Europe, China was living a sunny, orderly life, enlarged spiritually by a lyric poetry and a pictorial art whose beauties have only recently been suspected by the rest of the world. Followed another dark age, but nothing like so dark as the one Europe underwent, for under the Sungs art was by no means dead, only weakened.

The Mongol conquest at the beginning of the modern period brought China into its greatest epoch of world prominence when Cathay was the envy and admiration of Europe. The early Mings carried on by building Kublai Khan's capital, Cambaluc, into the modern Peking, one of the great art reservoirs of mankind.

Ch'ien Lung, whose reign marked the last pinnacle of Chinese civilization, and George Washington died in the same year, 1799. The ensuing decline was thus almost exactly synchronous with the rise of America. It is made easy for us to lose perspective and forget that when Li Po wrote his matchless lyrics, inarticulate Europe was struggling to repel the Saracen; that Wang An-shih was trying out his advanced economic theories while the Danes were ravaging England; that Kublai Khan's fabulous but no less real Cathay was a strong stimulant to the awakening imagination of the Western medieval world; that K'ang Hsi's classical dictionary was composed a half century before Samuel Johnson's brave but naïve pioneer effort in behalf of the English language; and that Ch'ien Lung was one of the most enlightened and surely the most efficient ruler at the time of the American Revolution. China's "sleep" has been but the short nap of a seasoned and vigorous old man, and excessive wonder has been expressed at his awakening, which was after all a foregone conclusion.

And now to return to the truism with which this paper began: the world for various reasons today is interested in

China. Why, we impatiently ask, has the republic not settled down in its fourteen years of war and chaos? Much of
the responsibility for these apparently futile years of trial
and error must be laid upon the rivalry and greed of foreign
powers, and upon that bugbear of Young China, economic
imperialism (which, after all, is no mere stereotype), with
its struggle for spoils, sometimes to be sure, under the guise
of disinterested philanthropy. Insofar as explanation must
be found in the character of the people themselves, one fact
will go far in evoking a more sympathetic understanding.
China has long depended for its government upon professionals. Time must be allowed for the people to develop an
amateur spirit in government; and since the Chinese are
such remarkable amateurs in the art of living, there is
abundant reason to predict confidently that with the increase of literacy, there will come the increased and more
intelligent personal interest in good government so essential
in a democratic state. Of course, literacy in itself is not
enough; it is of small benefit for people to read unless they
are provided with good things to read. Ability to read is a
doubtful blessing unless organs of public opinion are directed wisely and with good intent for the public weal, and
whether or not China's expanded literate public will be better served than the readers of America and Europe lies still
in the laps of the gods.

There is a rather widespread assumption, based too much
upon hasty observations of a people whose methods are so
unlike our own, that the Chinese are not good cooperators.
It cannot be denied that there is some disturbing evidence
of its truth, especially if one studies the official and educated classes. However, observations based upon a small
group at the top, for the most part tinctured strongly with
orthodox Western ideals of individualism, are not likely to
be just regarding the general lump. The returned students
have picked up the vices of Western thinking much more

readily than its virtues and are by no means the most accurate guide to racial character. Too many return to their native land the pampered darlings of a new system of thinking which leaves them stranded fish out of water, more cynical and hopeless than their teachers who have molded them. A truer indicator of a people's genius and tendencies is likely to be found in the common folk.

The Chinese people, individualistic though they may be, and trained in the school of hard knocks to look out first for number one as they most certainly are, have long practiced mutual aid in their daily living, and in this practice have developed a technique that will sooner or later be put to good account governmentally. This truth may be evidenced by many common observations, any one of which may seem trivial, but which in the aggregate have a good deal of significance.

Everyone new to China is astounded at the number of workmen habitually employed on small jobs. Five men will be engaged in the business of sawing off one limb of a tree; seven seems to be the normal number required to pull a small tennis-court roller; one small donkey pulling a flimsy wooden plow must have an attendant at his head and another at his tail. Western efficiency sees at first in this only Oriental laziness or ineptitude. I am convinced, however, that our natural first view is entirely unfair. The four hundred and forty millions must live; jobs must be multiplied; and the coolie is perfectly willing to do a day's work at low steam and accept a quarter of a wage, provided his brother and his uncle and his friend can have a like job and a like wage. A quarter loaf for each is better than a whole loaf for one, who would, of course, have to share the loaf with three jobless men and their families. To be sure there is a vicious circle responsible for the low efficiency of the Chinese coolie: men who are habitually undernourished are physically unable to exert the energy of a satisfied stomach.

Most heavy burdens are carried on a pole which rests on the shoulders of two men. This task requires a very delicate adjustment of step and minute bodily movement or it would be intolerable. I hazard the opinion that two big, husky beefeaters would be terribly harassed to carry in this way one of the immense watering tubs that two little cabbage-fed coolies sidle along under with seeming ease.

When a heavy sack of grain falls off a cart, one man will never attempt to worry it up on top again. Three will lay hold of it here and there, and with an uncanny instinct for the muscular applications of each other, will ingeniously twist it up into its place. There is always someone on hand to help. I suppose the Chinese have carried mutual helpfulness to the highest point it has ever reached; indeed it must be admitted that sometimes there are so many willing helpers that little tasks are impeded, but the triviality of the occasion and the occasional inconsequence of the help offered must not blind us to the significance of the fact.

Though there is sharp competition among ricksha men bidding for fares, or shopmen for customers, once the bargain is made, admirable cooperation obtains. Peking runners like to keep within a limited beat, and often to the disgust of passengers bargain en route with an idle aspirant to finish their run. I learned something of this system one day in going from Legation Quarters to Hsi Chi Men. Usually we took our special runners from Tsing Hua College into Peking and back — a distance of about twenty-four miles — but this day I had gone in by train and had to depend inside the city walls upon local talent. I was shunted into four different vehicles in going five miles, the fourth arriving at the last minute on the wrong side of the railway station outside the gate, just as my train pulled out. So I was forced to hire a fifth boy to take me home. There is no doubt, I think, that there was a dark conspiracy to extract tribute from the tenderfoot. For my part, I could not hold rancor; rather was

I forced to admire, perhaps not altogether gracefully, the technique of perfect cooperation fostered by the severe struggle for existence.

The whole game of "squeeze," so exasperating to the average tenderfoot, and from our viewpoint, so morally reprehensible, has at least the merit of fostering cooperation. When the houseboy tramples over your coal each time he fills the hod, he is making coal dust and insuring the coal-ball man a job and himself a commission. Thus, like Chaucer's apothecary and "doctour of physique," "each maketh other for to wynne." A systematic though moderate policy of sabotage is practiced in kitchen, garage, and all the various repair shops. The devotee of efficiency is maddened when the chair glue weakens, when the kitchen stove requires its monthly or bimonthly rebuilding, when the water pipes demand a too frequent exhumation, and when the valve caps of his bicycle are regularly missing after a trip to the ch'e p'u tzu. But philosophy will charitably assign the blame to the right source, over-population and under-pay.

Another illustration of a different sort. The Chinese are very fond of a species of acting entertainment known as huang liang or the "double-yellow." One actor in sight on the stage presents a spirited pantomime, while another, concealed under the table covered by a copious drape, sings or recites a historical ballad. This performance demands the nicest adjustments imaginable to prevent absurdity. The exactness of the timing and the general perfection of the merged halves of the actors is the test applied by the audience. I can testify from witnessing several such performances by student amateurs that the results are as amazing as they are charming. This is team-play with a vengeance. It is not surprising that youths trained in this kind of team-play should so soon develop proficiency in games like soccer and basketball, nor that they should organize such remarkable national movements as those of 1919 and 1925.

These illustrations must suffice. They surely indicate some racial training and skill in cooperation.

Sun Yat-sen is dead — just when his life work seemed to be approaching a successful culmination. Press comments on his communist tendencies held him before the world as an impractical idealist, self-deluded and deluded by every filibustering military and political self-seeker; a man who was out of touch with the slow, temperate Chinese people and one who consequently could have no deep hold on them.

I was in Peking when he was invited to attend the Reorganization Conference. He came by stages, through Japan to Tientsin, a very sick man, while the inimical press callously gave out that his illness was feigned for political reasons. He finally arrived in Peking with death literally staring him in the face and was very soon removed to the Peking Union Medical Hospital, where he underwent a series of the most drastic operations, not hoping so much to recover as to gain a respite of a few months in which to finish his work. But it was not to be. I talked with many students and teachers about him; I read all the comments I could find quoted from Chinese papers; I visited his bier where it lay in state in that part of the Forbidden City now opened to the people under the name of Central Park;* I gazed at but could not read the thousands upon thousands of memorials from all over China that lined the great avenues leading up to the audience chamber that sheltered his body; I attended with all the faculty and students of Tsing Hua College upon his funeral cortege as it passed along the highway to its temporary resting place in the Western Hills; and finally I climbed the many steps of the beautiful temple

*There was a strong movement to rename this park "Chung Shan" after Sun's popular designation, and thus associate the Forbidden City with the hero who raised the ban.

of Pi Yün Ssu where on the very pinnacle he lay, looking out over the broad plains of Peking. In every way possible I tried to experience and estimate the great soul of Sun Yat-sen.

And I believe that the spontaneous outburst of grief, north, south, and center, was an effectual answer to the foreign anti-Sun propaganda. On all sides he was honored as the First Patriot; there was no second. No one on the political horizon at present can take his place in the hearts of his countrymen. Feng Yu-hsiang, on whom a corner of his mantle fell, perhaps comes nearest to holding a comparable place. But the differences are great: Feng is comparatively an upstart, a soldier and disciplinarian of slender education, limited political vision, and tainted with the last two years of questionable vacillation. Sun was a *national* hero; college orators referred to him as "our father," a term in which all seemed to find spiritual satisfaction. He was everywhere compared with Lincoln, a comparison which in China, as in America, leaves nothing to be added.

Personally I believe that the reason for their love of him is that he embodied as no other leader in recent times this deep-seated instinct for preservation by mutual aid. Not Darwin only but Kropotkin also can find in this great people confirmation of his evolutionary doctrine. Sun saw a way to save China from its native vices by opposing native virtues. It is not what goeth into a nation, but what cometh out of it, that can save it. His slogan "China for the Chinese" was not merely a natural reply to "America for Americans" or "Europe for Nordics"; it was not a Boxer fanaticism directed against all things foreign; it was the deep-welling racial wisdom of a seer. He saw that many of the infiltrating foreign influences were aiding in the defilement of China, and he had faith that China had native virtue and force, which if allowed to work unhurried and unfrustrated would result in another age of glory. But he is dead. The

84

Reorganization Conference without him was impotent; and those who declared that Dr. Sun was the chief stumbling block in the way of China's unification are at a loss to explain the worse disunion that has followed.

My thought jumps across the Yellow Sea (by all odds the most comfortable way to cross this uneasy whale-road, for in a boat it is a too-long-extended English Channel).

Japan gives the impression today of a nation frustrated; a nation wrenched loose from ancient moorings and shoved on to the skidway of modern progress. It is now hurling headlong to its industrial debacle along with the rest of the industrial world, which, if saved at all, will be saved as by fire. There is visible, not only in the cities but also in the smaller towns, the same hurry, the same disinclination to wait, the same anxiety, the same utter lack of serenity that we recognize as the symptoms of Western "progress." Japan is burdened with a modern army and navy, a too rapidly increased population, and an alarming leap in the cost of living. Japan is nervous for its national welfare, even for its national existence. This, and not a deliberately aggressive design, is the real menace of Nippon; a nervous man, afraid for his life, is dangerous with his finger on the trigger.

China is threatened with a like expansion and a like frustration. If China repeats the history of Japan, leaping into full-flown industrialism within half a century, it will be a disaster to the world, a loss immeasurably great though we may conceivably never realize our loss. A quick lacquer of Western methods such as has been administered to herself by Japan in a frantic endeavor to compete with the other powers would certainly prevent the contribution that China might otherwise make to a world in need of rejuvenation. "China for the Chinese" has behind it more than the narrow, nationalistic, not to say chauvinistic motive; it connotes also the deep-rooted wisdom of the people. Left to

85

themselves, the Chinese would not be likely to waste and wantonly fritter away their natural resources by forced expansion, as America has wasted and is wasting her timber, coal, iron, and oil. And this temperate development would, I repeat, be no less a blessing to the world at large; perhaps its salvation.

That China is quite capable of developing her own resources is not without evidence. The Peking-Suiyuan railway, over a difficult terrain through gorges and mountain passes, was planned by native engineers and its building executed down to the last spike by native workmen. The Chinese are perhaps excessively proud of this unique feat in railroad building, but they are right in the assumption that the success of the experiment could be repeated.

The bearing of all this on Christian missions is of considerable significance and will demand careful attention, especially in the face of recent anti-mission agitation. According to the sponsors and fomenters of the anti-Christian movement which has been gaining headway since 1919, Western missionary enterprise plays the hand or at least plays into the hand of economic imperialism. This charge is unjust to the spirit of Christian missions and certainly to the real love and yearning in the hearts of many missionaries with nothing in their minds, as the phrase goes, "but Christ and Him crucified." Still there is some fire where so much smoke rises. Perhaps that very boast is the reason for their failure with Young China; they know too little beside Christ and Him crucified; they are naïve regarding the economic consequences of their peaceful penetration; they are committed to all the methods of the civilization which they represent, and they honestly but ignorantly assume that Western Economics will be as superior for the Chinese as they ardently believe Western religion to be superior. They are the apostles of progress and have no patience with the native religions and ethical systems which teach the gospel of waiting. It would be worth the while of the Christian church to throw off the aegis of military protection and go only where there is an expressed desire. If it goes elsewhere, it should renounce extraterritorial rights and proceed armed only with the words of Jesus; in no other way *can* it go with integrity. Moreover and above all, it should fearlessly uphold the Sermon on the Mount, even if allegiance to it requires its missionaries to denounce the infamous practices of foreign exploiters of Chinese labor.

The fervent aspiration of China is that the powers shall keep hands off and permit her to develop in accordance with her own speed limits and along a self-determined path. America, with comparatively clean skirts and with the immense prestige gained by the friendly acts of Hay diplomacy and the Washington Conference, has the diplomatic opportunity of the century. China has shown many indications that she understands the art of cooperation at home, provided her welfare is not ungeared by the selfish personal wars of this and that tuchun backed by this and that interested power. China is ambitious to join the sisterhood of responsible nations, and will cooperate wholeheartedly and intelligently with the power or powers that give a friendly sign at this moment. She is no longer willing to play the part of the lamb by reposing inside the lion; there must be mutual probity and confidence, or no burden can be lifted.

To be specific, America, like England and France, demands that before the concessions forced from a dotard and degenerate Manchu empire nearly a century ago be relinquished, the present republic, torn by internal dissensions and pauperized by the nefarious tariff restrictions imposed from without, should put its courts on a thoroughly modern, that is, Western, basis; and thus insure that the property and lives of American citizens will be safe. But China is unable to do this while she is terrorized by foreign police and bound by an inadequate tariff against the dumping of foreign goods, or "bads."*

Germany and Russia, since they lost their extraterritorial rights during the World War, testify that they have suffered no hardships or injustice from Chinese courts. On the contrary, the rapid comeback of German traders in the Orient owes something to their very helplessness, to the fact that they come now with no panoply of power and no recommendation but necessary goods sold at reasonable prices.

Let America make a large, friendly gesture of confidence such as the relinquishment of extraterritorial rights of American citizens, and China will be on her feet in a twinkling. The morale engendered by such an act on the part of any nation, especially America, would be incalculable, far reaching beyond its proper boundaries. Japan was on the verge of making this concession apparently, when the unfortunate events of May 30 took place. If she yet beats America to it, the Asiatic alliance that would inevitably follow might indeed fulfill the direst predictions of those alarmists who speak of the Yellow Peril. Japan has probably further disqualified herself by her backing of Chang Tso-lin in the fighting of the last days of 1925. Her needy and greedy hands may retain their grip in Manchuria for some time to come, but if so, she will forfeit all hope of the greater prize, the friendship of the Eighteen Provinces.

America has now a clear field. England and France are distinctly out of touch. Even America has forfeited something of the good will of the Chinese people through our diplomatic third-degree methods of last summer. Before the middle of July, when I left Peking, there was an unmistakably unfavorable reaction in the native press toward the United States. But still the huge bulk of the Chinese people and the majority of the influential student body look to America as a big brother. One positive friendly move might

*A disability only recently promised redress beginning in 1929.

easily forge an unbreakable bond between these two giant republics on the opposite shores of the Pacific and forever remove the nightmare fear of color war. This should not wait until it is "reasonably possible," as the Baltimore Conference and the missionary letter from Kuling to Secretary Kellogg suggest, but should be done now. Delay and shilly-shally in step with the other powers that enjoy the same so-called rights may quite thinkably result in another world war within twenty years which will bankrupt every nation on the globe — save China and Russia.

I have not before brought the Soviet Republics into the picture, but there they are, in the background — and every day the skillful and able ambassador at Peking, Karaghan, is forging another little link of confidence between his government and China. Given one more year for his genius to operate, aided by our superior, holier-than-thou diplomacy, the chain will be strong. Not because Feng Yu-hsiang can get a supply of rifles and ammunition across the Mongolian border — but because they need a friend. Russia also wants a friend and Karaghan is the ablest diplomat in Peking.

But while the Chinese might welcome any port in a storm, they have no delusions as to communism. They remain cooperative individualists, as they were in the time of Wang An-shih in the eleventh century. They still strain across the Pacific for the reassuring voice of Burlingame and Hay and Roosevelt and Wilson. Need it be pointed out that the recent trend of events in Europe renders it probable that even powerful America may in the not distant future need a friend? The American people want to qualify; the great majority of missionaries, who best know the sterling qualities of the Chinese, are anxious for the move; teachers and unshackled observers are almost to a man convinced that a helpful impulse must come from one of those who are fettering China's resources. These all vote Yea for a firm hand-clasp between two nations so similar in their pragmatic idealism. Those opposed are the exploiters of Chinese labor, certain news agencies, and the state department at Washington. Which will win? Here is one of the main sectors in the battle-front between civilization and chaos.

❦ ❦ ❦

Oh East is West and West is East?
And ever the twain are one.
We are all washed by the same moon-tides,
We are all warmed by the sun.

1926

Tao

An Associated Press dispatch of March 18, 1926, announced that Peking students, parading in protest against the government's accession to a foreign ultimatum, were fired upon for five minutes. Thirty-two were killed and more than sixty wounded.

Tao, Great Tao,
Hear thou
The murderous guns that slay
The sons of man —
The sons of Han!

See thou
The calendar blossom red
In May on the Yangtze Kiang,
June on the Pearl,
March on the Pei in a ghastly whorl!

Feel thou
The fevered beat
Of China's heart,
Earth's tremors under Chinese feet,
The quiver half a billion brains
Repress at thought of foreign Cains!

Know thou
Brotherhood hates and will avenge
Unholy murder!
Whether it lurks in lanes at home
Or stalks officially the highways of Peking!
That White Men's greed

Will poison love in White Men's seed
For flags that cover diplomatic crime!

Tao,
Dost bide thy time?
Thy way sublime
Is past our finding.
How, oh how
Will love grow strong?
By piling Pelion on Ossa?
Wrong on wrong?
Is this Tao?

A Chinese Trilogy

M ANY cities in China are more venerable than Peking, which is only a modern upstart among the
nation's capitals. Sianfu in the central province of
Shensi had a hoary history as the center of civilization in
the Middle Kingdom when Peking was first emerging from
the mist in the barbarian North. In a sense Peking is not a
Chinese city at all, but a Mongol hybrid with a later Manchu graft. The plains of Chihli (Honan) in the midst of
which Peking stands, isolated and self-sufficient, did not
come under Chinese domination until a mere two hundred
and fifty years before the Christian era.

For all that, no city is a better representative of that
great complex of phenomena known as China. The large
seaboard and river cities, like Shanghai, Canton, Tientsin,
and Hankow, are treaty ports and have been much modified by Western influence. Peking, behind its impressive fif-
teenth-century walls, the great gates of which are still pon-
derously closed every night, has almost continuously for
seven hundred years been the center of officialism, has
gradually collected the arts and crafts, the science and
learning, the cooks and customs of all China. In a real sense,
therefore, Peking *is* China.

Moreover, few cities of the world have had a more romantic history than the Pei Ching (North Capital) and
Peking's comparative recency only serves to point the an-
tiquity of the Chinese race. For authentic tradition has it
that long before the Greeks set sail for Troy, the ancient

NOTE. First published in the *Hamline Review*, February 1926.

city of Chi flourished just north of the present city wall. Certain it is that when the great Ch'in annexed the plains of Chihli, or Yen, as it was called of old, he laid waste this ancient city and gave the phoenix its first flight. Under Ch'in China (which owes its name to him as much as to its other etymological root, Chung Hua, or Central Glory) was first unified; from that time, under one name or another, one dynasty or another, the site of Peking has played a prominent part in the fortunes of the sons of Han.

I have made one inevitable reference already to Troy; there is a further natural comparison. Archaeologists have found some seven or eight city layers of Troy, the city of Homer being the sixth. Peking is similar though not so well preserved, for China does not take good care of its antiquities. Let me name briefly these habitations of the phoenix.

1. *Chi*: A small but thriving city dating from about 1150 B.C. Chi'en Lung erected a tablet near the Great Bell Temple, two miles north of the present Peking wall, on what he said was the northern boundary of Chi.

2. *Yen*: A city of the Han dynasty, at about the beginning of the Christian era, situated just south of Chi and including a part of the present Tartar city.

3. *Yu Chou*: A T'ang city farther south, and taking in a part of the present Chinese city. Its banners flew from the seventh to the ninth century A.D.

4. *Nanking* or *Yen Ching*: The capital of the Liao kingdom. The Kitan Tartars divided China with the native Sungs for about two centuries. These Liaos made Yen Ching a metropolitan city, enclosed by twelve miles of wall, from 915 to 1125 A.D. The name Yen Ching still persists and is used popularly to distinguish the Christian Mission University of Peking from the National Government University.

5. *Chung Tu*: The capital of the Chin Tartars, 1125 to 1234. The site was extended to the southwest and included the famous Peking racecourse.

6. *Khanbalyk* (*Cambaluc*): The grand creation of Kublai Khan, which Marco Polo familiarized to the Western world. The name became further corrupted into "Cathay." Kublai greatly enlarged (1264-1267) the city walls of Yen Ching and took in again the old Chi. Khanbalyk now became for the first time the capital of all China and took a place of prominence which it has never since yielded except for a few years under the early Mings.

7. Finally *Pei Ching*: The present city restored and molded into final form by Yung Loh, the great Ming builder. Its walls, the most impressive walls in the world, were strengthened and enlarged and stand today almost exactly as Yung Loh left them, forty feet high and fifty feet across the ramp. The north wall of Kublai was drawn in two miles to the south, so that the famous Bell and Drum towers, which stood exactly in the center of Khanbalyk, are now close to the north wall.

Since Yung Loh's time no important changes have taken place in the outlines of the city, though many dramatic events have been staged: the fall of the Mings and the coming of the Manchus, the renowned activities of the great K'ang Hsi and his greater grandson, Chi'en Lung, the capture in 1860 by the French and English, the sacking by the Allies in 1900 following the Boxer affair, the establishment of a republican government in 1911, a year ago the quietly sensational occupation by Feng Yu Hsiang, a little later the almost unnoticed eviction of the last Manchu emperor from his Forbidden City, sans household goods, sans extra clothing, sans title, sans everything but a paltry half-million-dollar pension. And finally, only the other day, Feng's reported second occupation of the city, when he locked up his second president within thirteen months.

Peking is not the official name of the Phoenix City. That honor belongs to Ching Shih, which means Spacious Plateau. The name by which it goes in foreign histories and geographies is less attractive than any one of its native appellations. Notice: Ch'ao T'ing, Imperial Court; Feng Ch'ieh, Phoenix Gate; Shou Shan, Best Place of All; Yu Yen, Dark Swallow; and Yen Ching, Swallow City, a current name that revives memories in the people, of long ago.

Surely a Phoenix City this! Flames, famines, floods, revolutions, new dynasties, new governments — none of these affect it. Like the patient, persistent, surviving race, it stands within its twenty-six miles of peace-exuding walls, yielding up its romance like a fading odor. Not long ago J. O. P. Bland, who has contributed many records of China's romantic history, revisited Peking and found its charm well-nigh departed. That may be true for those who knew the phoenix forty years ago, but fresh lovers, who know nothing better, still admire it. The needs of a pecunious, pseudo republic dictate the junking of the ruins of Yuan Ming Yuan and the hawking of the art treasures of the Forbidden City; foreign states have forced without treaty a city within a city; French financiers have built a street railway from Hsi Chi Men to Ch'ien Men. Perhaps the next creation to rise from its damaged romance will be an electrified, garnished, paved, and sewered modern city. At all events, whatever the plumage of the new bird, it is certain to be living and delightful, "the last word in human interest."

PEKING CATES

Though my lines have not fallen always in pleasant places and many geographic sectors have not yet swum into my ken — like Paris and Vienna and Palm Beach — I do not miss them exceedingly since our year in the environs of Peking. If Peking is "the last word in human interest," it is no less the last olfactory twitch and gustatory fillip in stomachic pleasures. Chinese cooks, say highly seasoned and well-baked travelers, are no whit behind the French, and every one of the eighteen provinces has sent of its best to the capital, where they administer to compatriot students and officials.

But a year cannot grow a gourmet. Not in a land where one may live for twenty-five years, dine well and intelligently every day, and then be surprised by some old, thoroughly documented native dish when he wanders a mile from his beaten track. Therefore, I proclaim my humble lack of pretension. Not for me to sing where one may get the best of this or that — where the duck is most delicate, where the bamboo shoots the tenderest, where the pao-tze the least porcine and most heavenly, where the birds' nests the most ethereal, where the Mandarin fish swims in the most luscious sauces, where the "Eight Precious Things" are most *précieuses*. I do not know, and I do not know how to conceal my ignorance if I pretend to know.

A lowlier but no less lovely task is mine, to chronicle the eats of the street, the common, every day, every way temptations to fall down and worship Jizu, the laughing god of the jolly belly.

First, then, we stop just outside the college compound wall as we start on the six-mile ricksha ride to Hsi Chih Men. Here is my regular market for lo-he-sheng, or plain lo-sheng, as my favorite vendor calls the plump, crisp peanut of North China that relieves the tedium of a long ride. Friend Shih, who pulls me cheerily and entertains me with his jolly, nonoffensive thefts along the way, likes these lo-sheng pickled in brine. But Shih likes everything. He munches a green roadside date or tsao-er, a hard, scrunchy pear, a meaty apple (meat is right), all with equal relish, and pays no attention to the lurking turbellarian, planarian, cestoid, or annelid. I envy Shih.

Outside the city gate the tired camel men are regaling themselves at the open-air restaurants with tea, millet soup, great slabs of golden yu-mi cake, larded with fat raisins, and, of course, chu-po-pus, little greasy dumplings filled

97

with bits of pork not quite so succulent as that celebrated by Charles Lamb. I enjoy the satisfaction of the patrons, but I am willing to take their meat vicariously, for something more to my taste is coming.

At Lung Fu Ssu near the pig market I find what I seek, the pai shu (sweet-potato) man. I hand him four coppers (not quite one cent) and receive an enormous sweet, as choice as the Jersey variety and boiled to a queen's taste. It reposes on a grimy saucer, but with the wooden chopsticks I make the sign of the cross and spread it out fastidiously on its skin. Ah, this is the life. I am not man enough for all of it, but the nearest beggar-boy has plenty of room.

After the business of the morning I find myself inevitably in Tung An Shih Chang, the main market of the Tartar City. I must be hard to please if I cannot make out a delightful luncheon while strolling about and taking in the infinite variety of the bazaar, for everything is here from rice-paste mannikins, molded while you wait by an artist of the first water, to precious jades; from cheap stone rubbings to priceless painting of the Sung period or unbelievable pottery of Han. First for lunch I select a choice mi-kan, whose tender flesh shrinks inside its comfortable, loose coat, an excellent first course. For my *pièce de résistance* I gaze longingly at the varnished fowls, chicken and pigeon and duck and bustard, and all the myriad of appetizing animal tidbits that deck the boards; not so interestedly at the manifold forms of bean curd that masquerade à la McFadden. But my courage is weak; moreover, I can get along without necessities if I may have enough luxurious desserts. Of these there are plenty. I enjoy most the sweet cookies with sesame seed encrusted and the rice-cake sandwiches embossed with a wise saying of Confucius or Lao-tze. Last I select a galaxy of shan li hung (red mountain pear). These Chinese haw apples, as large as a good-sized crab, cored and dipped into boiling sugar syrup and impaled on a thin bamboo, are, I maintain, the last word in street delicates. They will satisfy me until I get home to my supper of Peking chow mien (none of your Canton-American stereotype) supported on the side by lily roots and water chestnuts and in the rear by a generous dish of ice cream.

THE LIE OF THE LAND

Very new countries and very old countries are the same in their treatment of tenderfeet. "He was a stranger and ye took him in" is a Christian principle that all lands respect and practice, Wild West America no less than the hoary East. A crude country has crude methods of impressing newcomers, so crude that one hardly pities the unfortunate who falls for such coarse stuff; an ancient civilization like China has classic, tried formulas, selected through many centuries. To fall unconscious victim to Mark Twain or Bill Nye or the marvelous tales of the ubiquitous lumberjack demigod, Paul Bunyan, is something of a disgrace; but to kowtow to an Oriental liar is part of a liberal education.

Lord Bacon in his famous *Novum Organum* analyzes four species of "idols" or fallacies: *idola tribus, idola specus, idola fori,* and *idola theatri.* I shall follow his illustrious example and say a word in inverse order of Lies Theatri (official), Lies Fori (shopmen's), Lies Specus (house servants'), and Lies Tribus (friends').

As a foreword let me say that what I write must be taken with a good pinch of salt. A more charitable or a more enlightened view might not give many of the examples I cite such a discourteous description.

First, then, the Lie Official! The most obvious one is the government railway timetables, which are always, both in war season and out of war season, extraordinarily deceptive. Diplomacy, to be sure, lies in every country; the Chinese species differs in being more humorous than most. The recent appointment of Wu-Pei-Fu to the post of Commissioner of Waste Lands in Turkestan was a rich joke; still richer was Wu's reply—to the effect that he felt his small abilities unsuited to such an exalted position, but would gladly accept the post of *assistant* commissioner provided Feng Yu-Hsiang were made his chief.

China is an immense political stage today, swarming with accomplished military liars who fool not only the tenderfoot, but even those to the manner born. No one trusts any one else; treachery is the order of nature and scarcely to be distinguished from patriotism. Whether Feng is a traitor or a patriot will only be settled by the event; meanwhile the question offers as nice subtleties in argument as any metaphysical question of the Middle Ages.

In the market place money changing is the greatest game. In the business hours of any day one could, by working fast, reduce a million dollars to a negligible sum by selling and buying silver dollars. Ten exchanges each way would cut it in half; twenty-five would barely leave enough to buy a pot of tea at the Summer Palace.

Then the curio shops! How can one doubt the integrity of the dignified dealer who assures you of Chou or Han or Sung origin of the copper bowl that he has just dug up from the barnyard? If you object that so-and-so got a replica for a dollar and a half, he will blandly explain that so-and-so is his friend and offer it to you for five dollars. At the Ch'ien Men bazaar some dealers ask four mow for a little brass candlestick, expecting to take one and a half. Others ask only one and a half, and when a dollar is proffered give the innocent tenderfoot small mow instead of large mow in change, thus getting their thirty cents after all. On the notorious pseudo Marble Boat a pot of tea costs twenty-five cents; with three more cups and an extra dash of k'ai shui (hot water) the same pot costs one dollar. And so on *ad infinitum*!

The servant's home lies are usually relieved by humor.

The sewing amah who wants a day off for a jaunt to the city resurrects a grandmother with a sore leg. The first boy (chargé d'affaires), getting a bigger squeeze from black coal than from red, by some wizardry with drafts produces a horrid stench of coal gas from the red coal; and the tortured master gladly gives him an extra dollar to exchange the hoong for hei. The cook with whom the tenderfoot boards serves Australian tinned butter and much-watered milk until the mistress gets wise, when he cheerfully produces fresh, sweet butter and milk with the normal amount of butter fat. All in the game!

Finally the idols of the tribe, the friendly lies of one's kind, who tell tall tales to impress the tenderfoot and consolidate their position. One says soon after our arrival that we must be awfully careful to examine our shoes and beds for lurking scorpions, whose stings are "not necessarily fatal to anyone over two years old, but decidedly unpleasant." Another entertains us with stories of the 1922 campaign when Chang Tso-Lin's defeated soldiers camped outside the compound and *nearly* looted and sacked the place, prevented from carrying out their fell design by a five-year-old American boy with a toy pistol and some fluent Chinese.

All of them speak extravagantly of the weather of North China — reminding us of how we talk in Minnesota, to say nothing of Florida, Texas, and California. Already within two months we have experienced more cloudy days, more rain, and more disagreeable October cold than China has ever had in three normal years.

But the greatest sport of all is joshing newcomers about their delinquencies in bargaining and jeering at their first attempts at curio hunting. Their bronze is always brass (and in truth, so it usually is); their ivory, bone; their jade, green glass; their amber, celluloid; their Da Ming porcelain not earlier than Tsao Kun or Yuan Shih Kai at best.

It does not require a long residence to get the Lie of the

Land. But just when one begins to sense it at every point he grows aware that one of its most fascinating lies is this one — that it is all humbug; for it is not. No five-thousand-year-old people can be a humbugging people.

And the lie after all is only a pose — a manner of speaking.

A HUMANISTIC TRIOLET

Man the time-binder builds music and rime —
Arts, sciences, isms, playful, profound.
The animal space-binder ramps through his time
While man the time-binder builds music and rime.
The angels may cover eternity's round,
May live in an n-dimensional prime;
But man, the time-binder, builds music and rime,
Arts, sciences, isms, playful, profound.

Pai to Po

Meng-te has asked for a poem
And herewith I exhort him
Not to complain of three-score,
The time of obedient ears.

From "On Being Sixty" by Po Chu-i

Well Po, my ears are not so obedient.
They report, You are sixty: be your age!
You are no longer fit for tennis . . .
You cannot with impunity cut down a tree;
Each full ax stroke cuts off your own life span . . .
You cannot bear the over-load.
For heaven's sake, no, for your time-on-earth-sake,
Be your age!

So my ears hear,
But how can I obey?
A month ago I was not sixty-one;
I beat a cocky racqueteer of half my age
And didn't raise a sweat. Last summer when
I felled a giant white oak, I leaped
From saw, to ax, to wedge and mall, and back
Again to ax, and neatly laid "King Lear"
Exactly where I planned, along the hillside.
Sure, my heart was jumping — but it soon
Grew quiet. I've had that sort of fun
For sixty years. What is so diabolical
About the sixty-first? Let's make another billet!
Let's play another set!
— but sometimes in the course of a familiar

Loved diversion,
The hidden sapper strikes a dastard blow,
And my house quivers to its base.

What was your secret, Po?
I have your "character," your *tzu*,
Your name in common with the great Li Po,
But have not learned your wisdom.
Resentful at the flow of time,
The uncalled stations passed through in the night,
And not on any schedule,
The scenes and scenery I must have missed—
I make demand to have the trip run over,
Or my money back. I will not recognize
A *fait accompli*. No more did Cleon,
Whose works of art did not console him for
The loss and atrophy of rowing muscles.
I must be pagan still; and do not wish
To barter for a future, questionable joy
The present good, well-tested happiness.

And so I am a fool.
My name should not be *Pai*, "shining,"
But call me *Hei*, "full of darkness."

Yet, good Po, is it so wise to limp
And stumble down the last decade or so,
Rather than run full-course and in some last
Mad leap—which haply might be made—
Shatter the cup, and spill the wine
While still it bubbles strong?

August 29, 1942

"I Am the Captain of My Soul"

I T WOULD be a task worthy of Stuart Chase or any other eminent statistician to discover how many thousands of times within the last few years these brave words of Henley have been cited approvingly, even enthusiastically by religious leaders, as though they embody an ideal Christian spirit. Within the brief span of a month I have heard them chanted in chapel, declaimed by a devout college president, intoned by a minister in a sermon on Christian faith and by a United States senator in a great Methodist Men's Council.

> *Out of the Night that covers me,*
> *Black as the Pit from Pole to Pole,*
> *I thank whatever gods may be*
> *For my unconquerable soul.*

These are great words, ringing words. They conform to Coleridge's fine description of poetry, "the best words in the best order." I love them as much as those who love them most. But they are not Christian. They go back in their spiritual ancestry into the fogs of England or the land of Beowulf long before Augustine brought the message of personal immortality — and trust in a Heavenly Father. Said Beowulf on the eve of his fight with the Water Witch, "Wyrd often-times spareth a fated earl, *if his courage holds.*" If Henley had been in Heorot on that night in the fifth century, the meeting would not have broken up until they had sung with fine gusto,

NOTE. First published in the *Methodist Review*, March 1927.

105

I thank whatever gods may be
For my unconquerable soul.

However, every time I hear them injected into an orthodox
Christian discourse I wonder anew at the marvels of illogic
that can fit them into a sermon preceded by the Lord's
Prayer and followed by,

Sun of my soul, thou Savior dear,
It is not night if thou art near.

Every other phrase in the poem exudes the same bleak,
stark Anglo-Saxon agnosticism as well as the racial courage
that holds on "when there is nothing in him, except the will
which says to him, 'Hold on.'"

Whatever gods may be
(But there are no gods, he means.)
In the fell clutch of circumstance
(Where is the divine uplifting hand?)
Under the bludgeonings of Chance
(Not Providence!)
I have not winced nor cried aloud
(No hint here that "I will lift up mine eyes unto the hills,
from whence cometh my help.")
It matters not how strait the gate,
How carved with punishments the scroll
(No suggestion of repentance in the hope of having sins red
as scarlet washed white as snow.)
I am the master of my fate,
I am the captain of my soul.

It seems to me that a mistake the orthodox follower of
Christian tradition makes too often is to capture any worthy
sentiment or belief that exists or has ever existed, and affix
it to the tail of the Christian comet. All that is Christian is
good (?). All that is good is Christian (?). This has multiplied untruth in it. The modernist, intent on "saving" the

106

church from the dangers that beset it is perhaps the worst offender. He will make a complete list of all the virtues and all the ideals which to our age seem worthy, and calmly announce that the total is Christianity. He will go into the fogs of the nineteenth century for that magnificent creed of the honest doubter, Arthur Hugh Clough,

> It fortifies my soul to know
> That though I perish,
> Truth is so;
> I steadier step when I recall
> That though I slip,
> THOU dost not fall.

And without blushing he will identify "thou" in the last line with the Christian God, although it manifestly refers to Truth. He will with the best intentions wrench history to bring Epictetus and Marcus Aurelius into the arc — or into the ark. He will even commit the absurdity of making Laotze, five hundred years before Christ, a plagiarist when he said, "To the good I show virtue; to the evil I also show virtue, for Virtue is good." He needs a lesson from modern realism to teach him that claiming everything is likely to lose him everything.

Christian faith is built upon heroic stones in human nature. The essence of it is *love*. In the sophisticated Chinese of the sixth century B.C. was a serene perception of the virtue of virtue; it was not Christian. In the Greek Stoic was the hard endurance of him who said,

> Your ship is lost. What has happened? Your ship
> is lost.
> Nothing more? Nothing! Your son is dead. What
> has happened?
> Your son is dead. Nothing more? Nothing!

In the savage of North Europe was a furious individualism which still erupts in the nineteenth century in words that

107

stir everyone who hides close under his skin the same feeling that he is alone in the universe, and not afraid: "I am
the master of my fate." Christianity was none of these; it
was love. A Christian is blind who claims them; insensitive
to the contributions of other cultures and other teachers,
but stone-blind to the light in his faith. That light which
shines in the darkness of a brave but foolish and braggart
individualism is the wisdom of dependence, the gospel of
love, the doctrine of mutual aid.

We shall always thrill to the defiance of one who stands
alone and glories in his puny strength at hopeless odds with
the winds that storm the universe. That way lies heroism.
We cannot help the thrill if we would, considering our ancestors. But considering our descendants, we will look about
us, and perceiving other men beset by the same puzzlement
and chilled by the same isolation, we will draw together,
warming and heartening each other with our common lack
of heroism. That way lies Wisdom!

YOU SHOULDERING OAK

You shouldering oak, you bare, bleak, blighted oak,
Your leaves are early gone; we call you dead
No birds this summer choir-loft on your head,
Dazed and dismantled by a palsy stroke.

Yet vertical you stand. How strong a tree!
A man cut off must in three days or four
Take cover under ground — and evermore
A horizontal slow recession be.

While you, for many years with heart as sound
As when you flaunted color, stand your ground.

August 1943

108

From Reviews in the Chicago Dial, 1913-14

THE PLAYS OF STRINDBERG

TO UNDERSTAND and appreciate to the full Johan August Strindberg, one should be a late-nineteenth-century Swede, an *habitué* of Parisian society, a dabbler in all sciences, something of a genius oneself — and more or less divorced. Failing in all these qualifications, the present writer approaches his task with a humble spirit. He might even have been catalogued by Strindberg among the "right-minded," though I trust not. One may still love his wife (at least in America) and entertain an old-fashioned enthusiasm for marriage without deserving the epithet of "right-minded."

No one can read a play of Strindberg's without receiving an intellectual jolt. There comes the startling conviction that here is the transcript of a great mind. One may or may not agree that what one reads is great drama or great literature, but there is no doubt that the big, restless, cutting, probing spirit of the man who wrote it is a stupendous human spectacle. It is common for critics to see in Strindberg a type — the restless, honest pessimism of the last quarter of the nineteenth century, an epoch recognized by most contemporaneous philosophers as a "transitional era." This is true in a very real sense, and still I find Strindberg, of all recent writers, *sui generis*. Nowhere else have I come upon such utter desolate pessimism; but it is an earnest pessimism —

NOTE. In reprinting parts of these reviews of more than a generation ago the author fully expects to be "hoist by his own petard," for he has become increasingly conscious of "the pathos of distance."

there is nothing of the fermentation of the cynic in it. On every page is the nervous anxiety to find happiness, joined to the rational despair of finding it. The writer does not seem like a man who has turned bitter because his own life disappointed him (though no doubt that was tragic); his pessimism is biological, and so complete.

The Father and *Miss Julia* are the most important of the works under discussion. The extravagant encomiums bestowed upon the former will prove somewhat bewildering to many readers in America, especially those of the "right-minded" type. The play is saturated with the darkest misogyny. The theme, that no father is sure of his own fatherhood, is the final cause of the Captain's madness. The wife, who shows traces (but mere traces) of a type, is a creature who appears to believe genuinely that she is justified in her persecutions and harassments. Mr. Edwin Bjorkman, the translator, in one of his admirable introductions, says that Strindberg placed woman midway biologically between man and the child. But Laura, Woman Fighting for her Offspring, is not midway between man and the child; she is somewhere between ape and tiger. The whole thing lacks "edification," and fails to convince that there was ever such a silly, strong man as the Captain, or such a good, devilish wife as Laura; and it is at least an open question whether the play possesses enough truth to give it high literary value.

Miss Julia for construction deserves all the praise it has been accorded. Its unity and mass are admirable in their art — even if, like all art, they are a bit unnatural. The long and famous introduction by Strindberg is extremely interesting, and pregnant with practical suggestions in stagecraft. The translator, too, deserves the grateful homage of an English-reading public for an extraordinarily brilliant translation. I judge less than usual is lost in bringing the work to us from the Swedish. Take it all in all, *Miss Julia* represents Strindberg's peculiar genius in one of his most successful climaxes, so it is significant. Still, even *Miss Julia* does not quite bear out the promise of the elaborate introduction and the play's immense reputation. Strindberg admits, or announces rather, that he has made Julia an "exception to prove a rule"—a sort of thing, by the way, that seems difficult to square with pedestrian logic. Julia decidedly impresses us as an exception, and there are so many contributing causes suggested for her lapse and consequent tragedy that we are bewildered and chagrinned. Her mother's shady past, her father's foolish ideas of education, her own complex nature, her insulation against decent marriageable men, the license of the Midsummer's Night dance, her father's absence, Jean's superficial gentlemanliness — all these things, we are asked to believe, combined and brought it about that Julia most brazenly threw herself into the arms of an unimaginative boor and was afterward shaken by alternating currents of remorse, passion, ecstasy, and hatred, ending in the deepest self-loathing and, presumably, suicide. We agree that it may be true, but what of it? It merely goes to show that nature and chance and the author can form a combination too much for a human girl. Miss Julia is honorable — nay, more, noble. It is because of her nobility that her tragedy is a real one. Nevertheless, it is difficult to sympathize with those who find this play "too sad." Julia is too great an exception to feel sad over. It is very good realism, but it is not reality.

This brings us to the touchstone. Is there nothing but sex, sex, sex to write about? Why do all roads in modern fiction and drama lead into lovers' lanes? It would seem that we are more primitive than our ancestors, who could find pleasure in tales of friendship and heroism, sometimes omitting, as in Beowulf (a Swedish hero, by the way) the lady in the case. Our age has been sex-mad, and Strindberg is a symptom.

There is still another, and more vital, criticism — the vulnerable point I have above alluded to. Strindberg is big, but not big enough. He is courageous, but singularly fearful about the pain in the world. He never learned the lesson Carlyle beat into the head of the nineteenth century — that Duty, and not Pleasure, is the chief end of man. In his later semimystical plays particularly, such as *There Are Crimes and Crimes* and *A Dream Play,* the hedonistic philosophy is responsible for the pessimism. The tragedy of *A Dream Play* is the endless recurrence of duties. Personally, I shall reserve my pity for the man or woman who does not have this endless round of duties. God have mercy on the victims of the drug, dilettantism. The philosophy which cannot understand pain and suffering and duty in the world, but merely inveighs against them, is not big enough.

One play from his third, or "Symbolistic," period stands almost alone. This is *Easter.* There is a sweeter, saner, more life-giving spirit about it. I should like to believe that it represents without irony the older and riper Strindberg, but it seems to have been nothing more than an eddy, a moment of spiritual rest in his tumultuous life-and-thought stream. In this Swedish *Vicar of Wakefield,* where everything comes out right in the end, Strindberg says to the little child, the world: "Here's a quarter for you. Run along and buy some sweets with it. I know they will make you sick, but I don't care this time."

Somewhat similar in tone, though belonging among Strindberg's early work, is *Lucky Pehr.* It is an allegory that brings up many associations, chief among them being Ibsen's *Peer Gynt,* Maeterlinck's *The Blue Bird,* and Balzac's *The Wild. Ass's Skin. Lucky Pehr* is not unpleasant reading, but it contains no large or vital truth — except perhaps the incidental one that happiness comes from striving rather than wishing.

A sentence from Nietzsche appears at the head of a biographical note: "I tell you, you must have chaos in you if you would give birth to a dancing star." This is altogether apt for a volume of Strindberg's plays. You feel the whirling chaos in him, and he does give birth to occasional dancing stars. But the dominant impression one has on closing the book, on capping the telescope after a survey of the Strindberg firmament, is that a vast lot of star dust in chaos remains merely nebular.

THE PLAYBOY OF AMERICAN CRITICS

The Pathos of Distance! Is it merely a suggestive title, or is it a confession? Many readers of Mr. James Huneker's latest book will tend toward the confession theory, for despite the craft, perhaps even the genius, which has brought together these various papers written during twenty years, there is still an outstanding pathos of distance. They do not strictly make a book. The "mellowing of time," bespoken in their favor, is not always uniform, one must remember, for too frequently colors fade unequally. The subtitle, "a book of a thousand and one moments," is of course a genial and ingenious "tale of a tub" thrown out to divert the very sort of comment here made.

In one of the more recent essays, "The Playboy of Western Philosophy," the title is a boomerang which cuts shrewdly with a double edge. The "Playboy" is Professor Bergson; and he is a "playboy" because, Mr. Huneker says, his philosophy consists of beautiful images with which he dazzles our eyes and hypnotizes our judgment. The speciousness of this phrase proclaims its formulator himself as an image maker — and a maker of false images, too — for while there is much clever writing in the arraignment of Bergson, no understanding is evinced of Bergson's biology. "I recall a lecture of his at the College de France, though the meaning of his talk has quite escaped my memory because I was studying the personality of the man." Here is the confession of the phrasemaker: it is not necessary to understand a scientist, one needs merely study his personality. "The Playboy of Western Philosophy" is a clever title, but not a true one. So with "A Philosophy for Philistines," by which Mr. Huneker means pragmatism. Alliteration, that trustworthy servitor to phrasemakers, has here betrayed him, for it is evident from a reading of the paper that the writer does not credit the phrase.

But in a deeper sense this "Playboy" is a boomerang. His treatment of Bergson proclaims Mr. Huneker loudly as the Playboy of Western Critics. Having ramped genially over the pastures of art — music, and painting (including that thing called Impressionism), and letters — he leaps boisterously into the field of philosophy without troubling about the gate of science. Bergson's *Creative Evolution* is nothing much to him except an incentive to study the personality of the philosopher — which is human but not critical.

In "Matisse, Picasso, and Others" there is some real criticism which should be helpful to any who confess a curiosity in regard to that trio of phenomena, Cubism, Futurism, and Impressionism. Here the writer is at home; if one were inclined to be hypercritical, it might be said he is a trifle too much at home — he is utterly *négligé*. What, for instance, does this mean? "It is not alone the elliptical route pursued by Matisse in his desire to escape the obvious and suppress the inutile, but the creative force of his sinuous emotional line. It is a richly fed line, bounding but not wiry, as is Blake's." Here are perfectly good English words dripping from the pen of an artist and splashing over the ordinary lines of denotation. Such writing grows out of a doubtful conception of the purpose and value of the literary art. The art of writing does not exist mainly for the purpose of representing the other arts. It is itself the highest, and compelled to furnish copy of other copies it becomes degraded. Ruskin's "finest writing" was in his early so-called word-painting, of which we remember he grew ashamed later; his

114

finest writing, however, is in *Sesame and Lilies, Fors Clavigera,* and elsewhere, as he developed the deeper art of letters. So Mr. Huneker's best writing is not in the technical papers, but in the first story, "The Magic Lantern"; in "The Artist and his Wife," where he gossipfully proves both sides of his proposition; and in "Browsing among My Books," where he regales us with a discursive intellectual banquet.

But when all is said, Mr. Huneker *is* a great phrasemaker. His images are wonderfully felicitous, and for the most part fetching. He calls Bergson a "Yes-sayer," a term that sticks, like Mr. H. G. Wells' "Godsaker." Professor James, he says, wrote a "large, lucid, friendly book," and for this one comprehensive, satisfying phrase, hearty thanks! There are many such, for this is really a "book of a thousand and one moments."

NEW REPRINTS OF SAMUEL BUTLER

It seems fairly evident that the "seventy years of immortality" which Samuel Butler predicted for himself are now, twelve years after his death, well under way. This result has been brought about largely through the attractive new editions of his chief works which have been appearing at intervals for several years past. The most recent of these are *The Humor of Homer* and *The Fair Haven.*

The subtitle of the latter volume bears a forbidding aspect: "A Work in Defence of the Miraculous Element in our Lord's Ministry upon Earth, both as against Rationalistic Impugners and certain Orthodox Defenders, by the late John Pickard Owen, with a Memoir of the Author by William Bickersteth Owen." But let the uninitiated reader not be deceived. There is much juicy reading even here. This grave and magnificent fiction proves Butler to be the legitimate Elisha to those two eighteenth-century Elijahs of irony, Defoe and Swift. Indeed there is a very close connection between Defoe's *Shortest Way with Dissenters* and *The Fair Haven.* Both are works of ironical orthodoxy which had a success almost past belief. Humor must have been dead in the Church of England in 1702, that so many loyal souls welcomed seriously with pious joy Defoe's suggestion to hang every dissenter. And it must have been sorely afflicted in 1873 when Canon Ainger derived such comfort from Butler's argument that since Strauss admitted the death of Jesus and other heretics admitted that he was seen alive after his supposed (but fictitious) death, the whole orthodox position was historically vindicated. Forty years have passed; yet this book of theological controversy is remarkably up to date and is furnishing material for current popularizations of a view which in the medieval seventies must have represented its author, to the devout who chanced upon it, as a creature horned, hoofed, and damned. The editor points out in his introduction to the new edition an interesting relation between this successful irony and Butler's ob-security during his lifetime. Reviewers, he says, who had been taken in by *The Fair Haven*, "fought shy of him for the rest of his life. . . . The word went forth that Butler was not to be taken seriously, whatever he wrote, and the results of the decree were apparent in the conspiracy of silence that greeted not only his books on evolution, but his Homeric works, his writings on art, and his edition of Shakespeare's Sonnets." This opinion seems altogether plausible; something like the fact is antecedently probable in order to explain how a writer of Butler's force, humor, and perspicacity should require discovery by the generation following his own.

But even when handled by the most vivacious, theology has few charms for the present-day general reader, who cares very little whether Strauss or Butler or Dean Alford was right. And so the other of these two reprints, *The Humor of Homer*, will prove of immeasurably greater interest. A valuable feature is the memoir by Mr. H. Festing Jones, which though written only to do temporary service until Mr. Jones' full work on Butler appears, is nevertheless the best account of Butler's life at present available.

The contents of the volume, consisting of two lectures before the Working Men's College, London, one before the Somerville Club, and a number of short essays contributed to the *Universal Review* during 1889 and 1890, show Butler at his miscellaneous best.

As one would naturally expect, the three essays entitled collectively "The Deadlock in Darwinism" are the poorest. It is the anomaly of Butler's life that a writer of his humor and sense of proportion should have seriously devoted a large part of his life to pseudo-scientific haggling over Darwinism. Perhaps this is only a *post factum* judgment, incited by the fact that Butler, so modern in theology and art and criticism, is yearly growing more antiquated in science.

"Thought and Language" is better reading, as well as a more convincing scientific document, but it does not approach the interest we find in the papers on art, especially "The Sanctuary of Montrigone" and "A Medieval Girl School." In the intelligent levity which characterizes Butler's treatment of medieval church art there is nothing of the ill nature that one cannot miss at times in his controversies and also in his novel, *The Way of All Flesh*, where the fallacies are too close home to be treated with urbanity.

But let us come finally to the best. "For mere reading," says Butler in "Quis Desiderio . . . ?" "I suppose one book is pretty much as good as another." To this gentle judgment we must demur, for the first three papers in this volume are far and away the best "for mere reading" that Butler affords. True, *The Humor of Homer* contains something besides "mere reading." In it is found the core of his later work on *The Authoress of the Odyssey*, as well as considerations, not found elsewhere in his writings, concerning the broad humor of the *Iliad*, in its treatment of women and of gods. We may not here discuss Butler's attractive theory regarding the Homer of the Bated Breath, but we find it highly amusing, very saving to the face of the poems, and worthy of some serious investigation.

"Quis Desiderio . . . ?" and "Ramblings in Cheapside" are quite the most delicious bits of fooling since Swift's time. The comment on Wordsworth's "Lucy," in which from the information that Lucy's death made a considerable difference to the poet and the lines,

> *And few could know*
> *When Lucy ceased to be,*

he builds up the theory that Lucy was prosecuting Wordsworth for breach of promise; whereupon the poet, abetted by Southey and Coleridge, murdered her — this is altogether worthy of Isaac Bickerstaff and his prediction of the death of Partridge the astrologer.

There are three Samuel Butlers. "If *Erewhon* had been a racehorse it would have been got by *Hudibras* out of *Analogy*." Years ago the present reviewer tried to understand the bygone satire of the former, and for one whole term of school tortured himself by crawling out of bed at four in the morning to learn the *Analogy* by heart (ironical phrase, for the heart was not in the work). And with these superior advantages, he claims the right to prefer the Samuel Butler who wrote "Quis Desiderio . . . ?" to either of the others.

Durando

ACCORDING to Swedenborg, that most careful cartographer of heaven and hell, Lazarus must have had plenty of time — or whatever it is that corresponds to time — to be assigned to his permanent abode. Since he was an intimate of Jesus, he could scarcely have been a Tomlinson, one of those namby-pamby, would-if-I-might men that are not worth damning. Yet he must have been a very unsatisfactory raconteur, no doubt a serious trial to his curious friends. It seems doubtful even whether an Ecumenical Council or a Women's Institute could have tempted him to break the seal of his lips.

Jesus too had nothing to say about an experience that must have aroused in his hearers the liveliest curiosity. After all, such documents as those of the poet Dante, the seer Swedenborg, the poet-seer-mountebank-spiritists and all the host of fictional Morleys and Ligeas and Peter Grimms, interesting as they are in their way, have nothing of the appeal to men that would attach to the firsthand report of one who had been dead. That is why the case of David Durando has taken such a grip on me, all out of proportion indeed to the slender amount of factual evidence he was able, or willing, to give me. Of course, Durando's story will be taken by those who did not know him as another allegory or another hallucination. I should certainly not regard it seriously were it not for my knowledge of the cold, analytical, unimaginative nature of the man. I wondered at first why he chose me as his confidant, for there was little sympathy of a human sort between us. He interested me merely because I did not

119

understand him; he responded, I suppose, because all his emotions — save one — were intellectual. He would never have revealed himself to anyone who cared for him (if there had been such), or to anyone whom he suspected of a sympathetic interest.

Durando is permanently dead now and I think he would not object to my telling the story. A little more than a year ago his eight-year-old motherless boy was killed in a motor accident. In directing the details of the funeral he seemed as automatic as usual, though I thought he appeared relieved of some pressing burden. The next morning he lay dead on his day couch. The coroner could find no hint of organic trouble, no trace of poison of any sort, and so of course pronounced his death due to heart failure, occasioned by the shock. However, in the light of what Durando had told me before, the cause was quite otherwise, and it may be, altogether simple.

In 1920, just out of college, I was engaged as an assistant in the Bureau of Weights and Measures at Washington. My chief was a grave, taciturn man of forty-five, who had a reputation for super-normal accuracy and efficiency even among his associates in that exacting department. He had no friends nor human contacts in the laboratories, and during the months when I was trying to establish a foothold I had no interest in him nor he in me, except as a demigod of fact and a normally blundering neophyte. One of the other young assistants told me during my first week that "Old Durando" had been nearly drowned in the Potomac the summer before and had been a "little queer" ever since. This was about the only personal fact anyone ever mentioned about him, and the only reaction the incident had aroused was a mild satisfaction that a valuable machine had not been lost to the bureau.

Many evenings of that muggy winter I used to spend in

reading. Late one night I chanced on Andreyev's powerful story, "Lazarus," in a collection I had picked up that afternoon in a Pennsylvania Avenue bookstall. I was no novice to weird tales—could usually sleep soundly after a session with Hoffmann or Poe or Bierce—but this story had me going. The hour or so of sham sleep that I did finally manage to get was colored by the livid, bluish features and shot through with the baleful glance of the man who had lain in the grave four days. So next morning when I got to the laboratory ten minutes late after a gulp of coffee and two deadly "sinkers" my nerves were still jumpy.

Durando was on time of course, waiting to proceed with a piece of work on which I was helping him. I was in that state of mind when I would have confided in the sphinx or Woodrow Wilson or an Assyrian winged lion, and so not heeding at all my chief's terse rebuke, I started in: had he ever read Andreyev's story? did he ever think about the Lazarus incident? what effect would being dead for a time have on a man if he actually came back into the work-a-day world? and so on.

Old Durando's study presumably had been "but little on the Bible," but he knew who Lazarus was all right, for at the mention of the name he shot me a queer glance that probed easily to my medulla, and then a moment later he began to tune up the electric adjusters. All he said was, no, he had quit reading fiction (bad training, I think he felt, for a mind dealing in exactness), and he cut me short by saying curtly it was high time we got down to work.

The calm, satisfying self-reliance of the laboratory soon had its effect on me and my mind began to resume its ordinary functioning. But it seemed to me Durando was distrait. Once or twice when he failed to answer my check I looked up to surprise a stare of introspection in his slate-green eyes. One early afternoon a week later he looked up at me from his charts:

"I say, Pettigrew, about that Lazarus business . . . suppose you dine with me today."

When he added, "New Willard — Blue Room — quiet there
— six-thirty," I accepted with gusto. I was on time to a dot,
or maybe a dash sooner, and at first I thought I had beaten
old Durando at his own game of punctuality, for he was nowhere to be seen in the foyer. Strolling around the dim horizons, though, I discovered him hunched up in a big Sleepy
Hollow, lost in abstraction.

"Here you are," said I jauntily. "I was beginning to think
I'd have to dock *you* this time."

He looked up slowly, his eyes unwillingly withdrawing
from some fourth-dimensional object. It seemed to me he
was repenting of his unhabitual hospitality. But he arose
after a moment, and taking me perfunctorily by the arm
guided me toward the entrance of the Blue Room.

"No," he said in his ordinary staccato, "I shall be on time
until the end of the experiment."

There was something about his accent of "time" that
made me glance quickly at him to discover that his eyes
were glued again on that fourth-dimensional thing. When
the oyster cocktails came he resumed as though he had not
suffered any interruption:

"Time is a queer limitation, isn't it? Did you ever wish it
might be removed and we could test that new meter of ours
under timeless conditions?"

"Can't get away from the old Fourth Dimension," I said
flippantly, something to save my face since I didn't see any
sense in his remark. The courses came fast and good, and
we did little talking, restricting it to routine department
gossip. When the coffee and perfectos arrived I was in a re-
ceptive mood. Durando had eaten sparingly — I don't know
whether he really ate anything — and seemed no different
from the Durando of the office. He always appeared a
changeless, colorless machine, unconditioned by conditions,

and I suppose that was the reason that a healthy young animal like me looked on him with a bit of contempt. A man who could toy with such a dinner was inhuman.

It was just as well I was fortified for I soon got a shock that would have been harder to absorb before dinner. When my excellent cigar was going and Durando's was serving him as an invisible pencil and a dry smoke, he began abruptly:

"Pettigrew, you have heard of my experience in the Potomac last summer?"

"Yes," as I lolled back comfortably, "some of the boys told me you had a close call. Fact is," I smiled "Trystad told me you were under so long they thought the shark that cut such a wide swath along the Atlantic bathing beaches last summer had got you."

He shrugged in scorn of the childish suggestion of sharks in the Potomac.

"Pettigrew," he said distinctly, "I was drowned."

He raised his basilisk eyes and gave me a level look:

"Pettigrew, I *am* drowned."

My planked bluefish gave a great turn and I suddenly realized that I was out of my depth. I accepted Durando's strange words with an absolute conviction of their truth, only saying in an unfamiliar faraway voice, "Tell me about it, sir."

He began in his clear, clipped tones and told me the story.

"On the afternoon of Saturday, July thirty-first last, I went fishing according to my ordinary schedule on half holidays. A man must relax if he is going to keep taut. I started from the office when it closed, and my sister, who keeps house for me, was to bring my son Jonathan up to Hooper's Point at six o'clock to have supper together, after which she was going to catch the bus back for a bridge party, and Jonny was to drift home with me in the fishing dory.

"I have no friends. Jonny is enough; he makes up for everything"—a tiny flush appeared in old Durando's cheek and his eye glowed less green when he mentioned the boy —"and these little holiday jaunts are the pleasantest things life has brought me. My little son enjoys them too. In fact," Durando spoke almost shyly, "he seems to prefer my company to his aunt's or his playmates'."

It was later that I learned that this boy of Durando's had never really had a mother; he was the fruit of his father's brain and physical need. There must have been a woman, I suppose, but no one knew anything about her; she had passed out of the picture after fulfilling her physical function.

Durando had paused and drifted off into some domain beyond my ken. I waited a full half minute before I said, "Great institutions, these youngsters! My sister has a cute little Indian that thinks I am just about the cat's whiskers."

He resumed, ignoring my vapidity:

"I never believed in personal immortality—not since I was a sophomore in college. But the piece of a man that lives on in his son—that's different. There is something scientific, experiential. It has always seemed to me that Jesus would have come nearer to proving immortality if he had left a son who might have carried on his work, albeit with a reduced spark of divinity. What a pity, what waste of the highest life we have ever known, in his celibacy! I tell you, Pettigrew, he can't be a father's savior unless he has been a father; he can't be 'tried in all points like as we are' unless he watches through the night when a child of his seed fights pneumonia or scarlet fever."

Durando's cheeks showed more than a spot of color now and his fingers trembled slightly as they grasped the thin stem of his glass from which he took a nervous gulp of water. I remember reflecting that Durando had in him some of the stuff that makes the mystic—only it had ingrown and become curiously inverted. His enthusiasm passed and he relapsed into his habitual air of suspended animation as he resumed the story.

"On the afternoon I speak of I was somewhat depressed —vexatious things had happened in the bureau—Buckley had been made Assistant Director, a job I should have had, as every bureau man knew. Yet deep in my heart I wasn't so sure that I was really a better man. I had a sense of the bottom gone from everything, a sickening nausea of failure, some of the causes of which I could objectify, like my sister's heavy biscuit and over-boiled coffee, or my associates' jealousy and wire-pulling — but there was a goodly residuum which this afternoon pressed down on me as my own incompetence.

"Of course the war and the no less dark despair that followed the disappointing peace contributed to my general moral debility. Like every other more or less diluted American that summer, I was growing aware with sick surprise that we had lost the war; that liberal men and liberal ideas all over the world had lost their war, and the most disgusting thing about it to me was that I had ever been fool enough to permit war mania to raise my hopes of any good to come from such chaos — at least in my lifetime."

"Add one other fact and you have the mental stage set for what happened. I had just taken out a twenty-thousand-dollar life insurance policy, the kind that doubles the amount of the payment in case of death by accident. Jonny was the beneficiary. My mood hadn't been brightened by the obsession of this insurance writer, and when I looked at the crisp figures, my name, and the cold promise to pay under various eventualities, I had an ugly feeling that I was reading my obituary.

"Well, I was moping in the flat-bottom boat on the weedy shallows below Hooper's Point. Needless to say, in that dark mood, I had poor fishing luck; the bass and sand pike that inhabit that lush, rich feeding ground don't take to a melancholy angler. I was merely killing time until six o'clock when Big David and Little Jonathan would be together again. At a quarter to six exactly I decided to pull into shore and prepare the camp. I stood up to disentangle my line from a stout lily pad. As I lurched to my feet I must have given a queer side thrust to the boat, for it slipped back suddenly like a frightened hound, and I sprawled out flat on my face, slapping the water awkwardly and filling my nose and throat with thick bouillon.

"I'm not a skillful swimmer and had never practiced diving, so that the mouthful of mud must have paralyzed whatever aquatic instincts I had, and I gurgled slowly to the bottom among the lily stalks. At first I was frightened and must have taken in more water. The incredible had come upon me in a moment. I remembered a romantic story about a man and a woman stepping out of a boat in each other's arms and shooting like a plummet toward the bottom of the clean, blue Pacific, three miles below . . . Here was I, gasping in nine feet of muddy Potomac back-water slime. This wouldn't do, so I held my breath and tried to kick. My legs wouldn't respond; whether they were cramped or caught under a mat of weeds, I don't know.

"When I found my movements obstructed I suddenly gave up, without a struggle, 'yellow,' you might say. I resumed the thread of my gloomy reflections of the afternoon. The irony of fate, I thought. My life was a drab and bitter thing, with hardly a trace of what makes other men's lives rosy at times — and sweet; I was unlovable, undramatic, a clumsy marionette for the forces of life to try to magnetize; Washington bureaucracy was rotten, the peace was rotten; the world was rotten — what more appropriate end than this, alone and easy and without éclat! I was tired . . . No one wanted my contribution. An accidental death had never occurred to me as among the possibilities for one in my staid position . . . Here it was, at my nose, with double insurance for Jonathan, forty thousand dollars, plenty to assure him a future, a future unpoisoned by a bilious, gangrened, disillusionized old cynic whose hand was against all men's hands.

"What you have read of visions of sudden death, how the whole life history passes in review, has not been exaggerated. When the hammers began to beat in my brain, the result of the accelerated heart action, I saw my dreary life panorama, lightened here and there with its poor victories, hardly won. I shall not bore you with a full rehearsal of all that; you have plenty of imagination. After an aeon of autobiography I came to the present, to the fine reforms I had been planning and, but for blundering, thick-skulled superiors, would have instituted. I pitied myself and the world for their failure to take material form; I knew they would never come off now . . . The pangs of strangulation took a stronger grip on me . . .

" 'Lord, lord, methought what pain it was to drown!'

The words of the Earl of Clarence came back to me from student days:

What dreadful noise of water in mine ears!
What ugly sights of death within mine eyes!
Methought I saw a thousand fearful wrecks;
Ten thousand men that fishes gnawed upon;
Wedges of gold, great anchors, heaps of pearl,
Inestimable stones, unvalued jewels,
All scattered in the bottom of the sea:
Some lay in dead men's skulls; and in those holes
Where eyes did once inhabit, there were crept,
As 'twere in scorn of eyes, reflecting gems,
Which woo'd the slimy bottom of the deep,
And mocked the dead bones that lay scatter'd by.

"And then I jeered at myself: no such gorgeous setting

for your drowning. Here you are, tangled in a mass of rank river weeds, drowning like a rat in a sewer. That obscene phrase and the accompanying image was in my ears and eyes for a long, long time, while the hammers rang on brain anvils and each crash hurt as much as a blow on a raw nerve. And there were myriads of crashes. I had spent a day in the Bethlehem Steel Works once, and another at the Ford Plant in Detroit; my head was both of these telescoped into one hell of din.

"Finally my head became easier and I was relieved to think it was nearly over. After all, the actual dying, I thought, is not so bad; if my heart had only been less efficient I should have been saved all that torment. Now I shall glide off — and I was gliding, when — God! Six o'clock! Time for Jonathan to be here. Some one will pull my empty, terrifying carcass out of this slime for Jonny to look on, Jonny, coming to meet his daddy, his pal. He's coming to meet me, and he'll find a drowned corpse.

"The image of my little son's horror-stricken face when confronted with that morbid likeness of his father, his grief without me to help him get adjusted, dashed its force against every neuron of my brain. I must have given a tremendous, freeing kick and fought my way to the surface. But I was too far gone. I went down again and glided out entirely."

"You mean you lost consciousness?" The words oozed thickly from my throat.

Durando smiled in that ghastly way he had. "That depends, I suppose, on your definition. The evidence shows that my heart was still for something like fifteen or twenty minutes. It was not later than 5:46 when I went under. Some minutes afterward a fisherman drifting down the river saw my empty boat and my floating hat. He thrust about nearby with a pole and chanced to get it under my armpit. My arm clamped on it and he drew me up, already fighting to start my lungs. He told me the next day that my heavy, watertight watch was trailing by the chain when he brought me up, and he noticed the time particularly; it was twelve minutes after six."

"But this is incredible . . . nearly a half hour under water . . . five minutes is the limit . . ."

"It wasn't a half hour, Pettigrew; it was a year, maybe a decillion years that I waited for the touch of that oar . . . the human will is nearly supreme."

Durando's next words came slowly, almost painfully meticulous: "Once I have endured the pangs of death; I shall not need to face them again. At the proper time it will just be a matter of letting go. For myself the effort was a mistake, but when the proper time comes, when my return will not be distressing to Jonny, then I shall be glad."

I was still under the spell, seeing nothing ridiculous in the question, "Did you realize that you were dead during that time — or eternity?"

Durando's face was perfectly expressionless, and so his voice as he replied,

"Do the living know when they are alive? In passing from actual facts to created fiction, from the world of actuality to the world of imagination, the artist, or the scientist, for that matter, seldom knows just when he crosses the line, I suppose. His fiction is truth, and that is more than can be said for some of his facts . . . There was a difference . . . I cannot tell you . . . I am sometimes restless to return . . . death is just the law of gravitation, biologically conditioned, just a returning."

"Is there any difference now?"

"No," said he somberly as a ghost, "that is the hell of it. There is no difference. I see my life as a finished whole; there is no future to it, for I have tasted eternity. My work is finished and now there is nothing in me except the will which says to me, 'hold on! bide your time! . . . bide your time!'"

Slowly he arose and I with him as though moved by the same hidden lever.

"Goodby, Pettigrew!" That was all, no word of conclusion, no explanation of his singular confidence, no hint of purpose, no drama. Only "Goodby, Pettigrew," and there was never another reference to the subject by either of us.

Naturally I reacted for a time and called myself an ass for giving heed to such a febrile story, but I ended by believing it. Now as I said before, Durando has let go — returned. There was no heart trouble, no "trouble" of any kind. Jonathan was gone; David had no motive for setting his will against the law of gravitation.

A Fragment

In the *April 1914 issue of the* Forum *there appeared a rather long essay entitled "The Art of Everlasting Life," which, assuming a validity in mankind's very common need for a belief in immortality, undertook to follow a line of argument based upon the Christian scriptures and a modern acceptance of the general theory of evolution, resulting in a rational suggestion of conditions for the attainment of such a life.*

In contemplating this volume I thought at first that a reprint of that essay might be justified. Several friendly readers of a new generation, to whom I submitted it, thought it was not outmoded and showed some enthusiasm for it; others were doubtful; and their doubt I came more and more to share, with the result that, regretfully, I confess, I omitted it from the sheaf of manuscript first presented to the publishers. Later, in rereading Chapter 11 of Somervell's abridgment of Toynbee's A Study of History, *I fancied I discovered there in Toynbee's discussion of the creative acts by which individual human beings develop personality a point of view parallel with that 1914 essay. I was emboldened to reconsider, with the result that though I am forced to hold to the view that "The Art of Everlasting Life" is too long and somewhat otiose for readers of 1948, I believe it contains one fragment which I should like to see escape for a time the bonfire which the rest of it deserves.*

Section V ended this way: "An old evangelistic slogan somewhat in disrepute, but owing authority to mankind's highest priest, enjoins, 'Ye must be born again.' It is now my aim to suggest that this injunction with a new interpretation, is consistent with scientific fact and the most tenable hypothesis for personal immortality."

Section VI follows.

BRIEFLY resuming: there is no clear evidence for, and no spiritual purpose discoverable in, immortality for the plant or the starfish; there is a wider chasm between these forms of life and the higher mammals than between the dog or horse, and man. If universal human immortality is postulated, these higher mammals must be included; there is no possibility of avoiding this dilemma. Finally, the difficulties are considerably greater in assuming a personal immortality for all animal life or for all above a certain arbitrary species than in giving up the assumption of universal human immortality.

Consistency requires another step — the possibility that a man may travel through life without finding a soul and die with no prospect of any sort of life beyond. This is the step that all the preceding ones have been leading toward. Immortality for all of mind claims too much; it reduces to an absurdity on both sides; and is moreover not strictly immortality, but *eternality*. Eternality of mind, surgence and resurgence in the ocean of mind at the background of the universe, leads direct to a materialistic monism, the position of a less important wing of near-atheistic science and certainly far from the sympathy of theists. If the soul is eternal, not only will it never die, but it has never been born — has existed from the beginning with God and the universe, a view which makes individual responsibility, the potent watchword of religion, rather grotesque; for why should an eternal soul, coëval with the universe, be judged on a few breaths of time, when it chanced to be lodged in a body? So I submit that a variation of the old-fashioned view of soul as something distinct from mind, or rather a faculty or function higher than mind, though evolved from it (a conception surely not at odds with the evolutionist), is more probable on the whole than the more naturalistic dogma which we have just examined.

Let us put it definitively: the soul is a developed function of mind. I imagine we may think of it as the perfected fruit of mind, which after fruitage draws the total mind of the individual into immortality. When a man develops a soul he lives forever; when he neglects to cultivate this possibility of the infinite within him he dies forever. Physical birth is the first step toward physical death, but the birth of the soul, what Jesus referred to when he said, "Ye must be born again," is the first step toward immortality.

VII

Permit a geometrical digression in the interests of clearness:

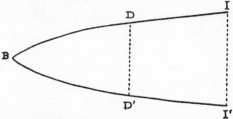

Suppose this simple figure to represent man's life. B is birth or beginning, soul-possibility, but soul-zero. (A traducianist will not be satisfied with this, but so much the worse for him.) We stand awed before this greatest of miracles and can do no more than recognize in it the great, constant, eternal act of creation. The diverging lines represent the development of his life — its ever widening interests, never drawing in nor forming a self-sufficient circumference, but ever spreading, spreading, aspiring to new, more, better life. The man with arms stretched out to heaven is its symbol. Now let DD' represent physical death. Shall that flimsy curtain stop a vital creature who has justified his creation by constant enlargement, has steadily maintained his life outgrowing, and is just beginning to sense the purposings of his Creator? The idea is repugnant, and what is worse, bad geometry. His life-parabola will continue to diverge toward infinity; this man will have achieved immortality.

Now another figure:

133

When the life, beginning as it must in physical, ingrowing interests, never transcends them, it must follow the circle, contracting around, self-looking inward on its own desires — and death, the perfect transmitting medium, finds little life to converge. Perhaps the soul has become a zero quantity even before physical death. The grave indeed then ends all; the perfect ego is a perfect circle. This man may have been called wise in the councils of nations, or may have counted millions by the score; but in bearing his Sisyphus load through life he has neglected to cultivate the flower of the soul, and death leaves him at the soul level of birth. In gaining the world he has lost his soul. Birth found him a possibility; death, an impossibility.

One more figure:

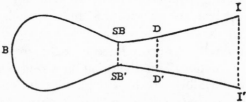

Here is a more unusual but quite possible optimistic curve. Here is Jean Valjean, Markheim, Jerry Macauley, and every genuine devil or egotist who turned genuine saint or servant of mankind — possible, "though as by fire." The point SB represents soul-birth, an altogether noticeable epoch, possibly narrowed to a moment, in the lives of many emotional people. What is called conversion, a change of direction in the curve, readily made in youth or early maturity, becomes increasingly difficult with the added years, until the time comes when a generous impulse must fight to break through a crust of selfishness deposited by years of consistent acts and thoughts.

VIII

We begin now to draw the threads together. Paul in his letter to the Philippians speaks of working out "your own salvation." This phrase has much significance here. To work out our own salvation, to be born again — are these merely pious phrases or may we clearly fit them into the scheme of evolutionary development? I believe we can.

Reverting now to the question, When does the soul begin?

If this line of thought is in a right groove, the soul begins when a man or woman actively, though perhaps unconsciously, follows love, rejecting self-love — chooses an interest wider than his own — decides to cleave to the good and despise the evil; the soul grows only if he stubbornly maintains that course to the end. The "chief end of man" is not "to glorify God and enjoy Him forever," but to serve God and man, or God in man, and thereby work out his own salvation, which is life. The best reason for time is eternity. Man is a soul-hunter. For this end he was born; not to shear sheep on the hills nor lambs on the stock exchange, but to win an immortal soul. And just as pleasure cannot be chased, but must always follow those who flee from it, so the soul cannot be attained by aiming only to attain it, but by eyes directed otherward and hands seeking to help someone not ourselves. Refined and self-conscious soul-hunting thus fortunately defeats its own purpose, while the robustious, unconscious *doers* who may be happily ignorant of the language of sweet idealism but normally interested in the Common Good enlarge the soul to its mysterious possibilities.

As to the evolutionary origin, the scientific rebirth:

The soul, let us say, is a transcendent possibility dependent upon a high order of mind, the type of mind that is found probably only in man. Every man has the necessary prerequisites to a soul, but he does not develop it *ipso facto* that he is a man, but only when he chooses and pursues consistently the Common Good.* If one of the Elferfeld

* When this essay appeared originally, I used "righteousness" where I now use the "Common Good." The former is open to the charge of ambiguity and perhaps of begging the question.

horses or any individual member of the higher species of mammals can be shown to possess a willful moral consciousness, there can be little objection to regarding it as a candidate for immortality. The small indeterminate variations of Darwin have been important in evolution, but they are not the only method of development. He himself admitted and recent biologists insist upon other larger, *determinate* variations — triumphant advances not explained by natural selection, like the short-legged sheep and the human eye. In other words, science demands the bridging of chasms in biological development, chasms that require suspension cables thrown from one side to the other with no intermediate abutments.

Pragmatism assigns to each individual some part in the construction of the universe, and this essay suggests that his chief creative act is the leap to a soul. Physical and mental evolution, preparing the way, bring man in his intricate life sheer to the chasm. He may walk safely on this side with selfishness to death. Beyond — is a soul to be gained by abnegation and service. "What shall I do," he cries, "that I may inherit eternal life?" Said Jesus to the rich young ruler, "Sell that thou hast," but we recognize in this reply the physician who is wise enough to prescribe individual remedies to particular cases. To sell what I have and give it to the poor would enrich the poor no more temporally than it would enrich me spiritually. "What shall I do?" is the question of the ages, and there is no specific reply. But we must flash the message, and hearing the answer we must boldly do. The soul is not super-natural — certainly not; it is only supra-Darwinian. By our own determinate variation we may pragmatically add our souls to the sum of the world's good.

Are You There?

LETTERS TO M. V. W. (1846-1927)

November 26, 1931

DEAR MOTHER: This is your birthday. Five years ago you
were with us when we celebrated your eightieth. That also
was a Thanksgiving Day. At intervals all through your life
your anniversary and the national holiday came together
and made us doubly glad. In truth November 26 was for me
every year a Thanksgiving Day.

But now it is hard to realize that nearly five years have
passed since I talked with you, and I have never since that
bleak February morning when you slipped away from us,
written you a letter. It seems now I cannot quite forgive
myself for such negligence. Every week since I first left
home at fourteen, except when we were temporarily together, I had written to you and you to me. You were sometimes
tired or ill, but you wrote anyway.

Why have we not corresponded lately, Mother? Of course
I have been busy and distrait; but busyness and distraction
are poor excuses. You, however, formerly were never too
busy. Surely your beautiful spirit is not always engaged in
adoration, or contemplation, so that you cannot find time
for homely talk with your children. At all events, I am going to begin again. Uncle Sam may not yet have completed
postal arrangements with your country. Come to think of it,
though, Edison has lately emigrated there, and possibly he
can do something from that end to improve communication,
though the chances are against him, since William James
and Sir Oliver Lodge have failed pretty dismally.

On second thought, I suppose you really don't have time

to write, for you have no *time* at all. You have nothing but eternity. And you have no *place* to write; all you have is infinite space. What a true embarrassment of riches! A somewhat limited heaven would be ever so much more comfortable for you, I should think. Certainly more pleasant for your children and friends if they could as a result have an occasional line from you. Sometimes I fear you may not be enjoying yourself as much as you used to expect. I recall how once you spoke not so confidently about the prospect of being draped in so much eternity, and how you hoped there would be in heaven something for you to do.

Now I find myself wondering whether you have experienced anything approaching your dreams. After trying to imagine what it might be, I am afraid you have been disappointed. Certain occupations are out, of course. Knitting and mending and fancywork I just can't believe God would plan for you, although you always got a lot of pleasure out of those useful pursuits. Still, God knows you got enough of them in life. You used to be uneasy when people praised you — as they did too seldom. So I imagine you have too high an opinion of the Good God to presume that He will enjoy listening to endless praise, even from such sincere and good people as you.

November 26, 1940

DEAR MOTHER: Here is your birthday again. I call it nine years since I started this letter; what do you call it? Scarcely a split second! Since you left, the astronomers have multiplied the universes and extended the Universe something scandalous. Do you remember that the last time you visited us we were trying to understand curved space? Einstein began publishing in 1905 for those who had ears and eyes. It was twenty years before we got even an inkling of what he was about. . . . We are still getting light from a star that blew up before King David was born. And we are trailing far behind and below the scientists and mathematicians who live in the funny icosahedrons above our sphere. I recall how Milton, though he knew Galileo personally, and fully accepted the Copernican system, nevertheless constructed his universe on the old Ptolemaic plan. That was nearly three hundred years ago, but if you would allow me to bet, I would risk a year's salary that plenty of people can still be found who think the earth is at the center of the visible world. . . .

It would be great fun to have you in the family again. I cannot feel with some spiritually minded that you *are* here. Do you know that for months after you left us I "heard" your bell tinkle in the night, and many a time I was out of bed and halfway to your room before remembering. I have not heard the bell for a long time. But I have no doubt that you are *there*. Next I reflect, "How do you want her here? As she was in the old time? Full of pain and anxiety and compassionate yearnings?" No, I could not wish the terrors of 1940 upon you. "Or as a visitor from eternity?" Well, yes, that would be fun — if we could learn how to treat you. . . .

November 26, 1941

DEAR MOTHER: Tonight I have an unwelcome reminder of you — though even an unwelcome reminder of you has its pleasureable tang. That familiar gesture, putting your hand — was it your right or your left — to your neck when it ached. I have that same kind of ache, I guess. My left hand goes up — and I believe it was your left hand. What a curious business, this heredity! The biologists who have knocked out so many of our traditional ideas about heredity, laying the phenomenon under question to environment rather, imitation and whatnot, would have a tough time explaining why it is the nerves of the left side of my neck too that squeal. Here you have been gone thirteen years, but you still tell me where to soothe my pain. You were lefthanded,

139

and though you were careful to teach me to do everything righthanded, I am pretty clever with my left at anything I try. . . . As I grow older I see oftener and oftener traits of Father too. Do you remember how we used to charge him with making up yarns and not knowing whether they were fact or fiction? I don't think my fancy carried me in that direction when I was a child, while I was under his direct spell. But in my adult life I have been sometimes embarrassed at a doubt whether a memory is a memory of an actual fact, or a memory of an imagined one.

November 26, 1942

DEAR MOTHER: Here we are around to another Thanksgiving Day, which falls again on your birthday. Since my last brief note I have suddenly jumped a sizable age span. My vital grasp was loosened last February by a set-to with bronchial pneumonia, and with the drugs they gave to get me through that. I can no longer reject the idea of growing old.

Since I first wrote you in 1931 I have covered a good deal of thinking territory. It has not been a happy time for the earth. "Chaos" has been the word almost constantly in my consciousness. "Chaos in the cosmos" is the theme of my annual poem (save the mark) since 1933 as I have watched the storm gathering for what we brag on now as a "global" war. But a part of my misery has been, I think subconsciously, because of the relaxing of my faith in the meaningfulness of these letters to you. *Are you really there?*

Probably it is necessary to believe in a personal God if we are to hold with the continued life of the individual. When I wrote "The Art of Everlasting Life" nearly thirty years ago, I had a weakened faith in a personal God, but I retained a rational belief in the possibility of life beyond death, a conditional immortality. Since then I have stubbornly tried to hold that faith, but with less and less assurance that there is a kernel inside the shell. The old cynical argument for believing in immortality, that one has nothing to lose and everything to gain, doesn't appeal to me. I may be in for damnation, but I'm not going to be damned for that particular stultification of my conscience. I am now certain, not that there is no reality corresponding to a personal God, but that to me the concept no longer makes the same kind of sense it once made. There is a vast difference between "a personal God" and "the personality of God." Since God is the soul of the universe, He has, of course, the personality of the universe. But it seems clearer that it is meaningless to cling to the hope that you and father and the thousand generations of our ancestors since the last Ice Age continue to have a conscious individual existence.

I am reversing the ordinary process. As I have read and observed the tides of human skepticism, age brings conservatism, recurrence to the comfort of old faiths. Youth has its fling, but middle age congeals the flighty blood and its channel takes the course of least resistance. The church spreads out its arms to the quondam skeptic. As the earth cools, its parasites crowd closer together for mutual warmth. Growing miseries of age tempt them to revive solace in the idea of future joy; they can thus better endure the inrush of narrowing horizons.

Occasionally I feel that I might be "happier" that way — just as I used to be tempted to believe that I might get rid of sciatica if I could only be fool enough to swallow *Science and Health*. But I couldn't do that then, and I can't do this now. . . . So, Mother dear, I am giving up these letters, along with the hope of seeing you again. If I am all wrong and shall hereafter actually feel the comfort of your presence anywhere but in my disordered brain, what a delightful surprise! I hope I'll have the grace not to act disgruntled at being proved wrong.

I am minded to turn aside here into one of the many bypaths that discussions of "faith" inevitably lead to. Does my belief about your conscious life or my conscious life have any influence upon its reality? To put it in another form related to the kind of cynicism I referred to a moment ago, is it possible that a disbeliever should discover after death that he had been wrong, and that he is a candidate for *life*? You remember I quit assumptions of hell, eternal punishment, a long time ago; so it is either *life*, or *no life*, depending on whether the individual was following in life a parabolic, outward-looking curve, or was riding a circle, an inward-looking, self-annihilating curve. Faith believers, except those of the hell-fire variety, assume that it is the faith that creates the thing. It would be to them a gross and brutal paradox if one who rejected a conscious good after death should discover after all that there is such a good and that he is eligible to it. Well, my mind is so constituted and conditioned at present that I must believe that such an important fact has an objective reality, or none. My reasons for trying to live an actively "virtuous" life have nothing to do with a hope of future reward. But if I am all wrong about life in eternity, the Good God will, I think, give me my reward whether I am expecting it or not. And if He has other views, that is all right too.

Returning from this speculation, I am thankful that you conceived and "had" me, and that I had you so long. Those memories are all the more precious since I cannot continue to trust in their everlastingness. I am glad to believe that you cannot know the pain of looking down on the dismal show the earth is putting on in 1942. At the same time I want to go on record as believing that there is an even chance that the earth-world will eventually feel a sense of relief, for a season, at its purging.

July 22, 1945

DEAR MOTHER: We have almost completed three more

revolutions around the sun since I wrote you my valedictory — as I then thought. At that time I was trying to reconcile myself to an abandonment of any hope of communication with you. Yet today my mind turns with a living thought to you. That you can think of me I have no more assurance than I had then; but it is amazing that you live so vividly in my mind. To be sure, that is a kind of life beyond life, and whether or not it can be a comfort to you thus to live in our love, it is a comfort and blessing to us. And moreover, you live in the memory of our sons. I presume their children will hear them speak of you as they look at the records in the old Beyer family Bible, and our sons may still carry childhood recollections of the "Grandma" whom they tenderly loved. But personal tenderness can hardly carry through into the next generation, to their grandchildren.

I have one final — we shall see — thought about your *being there.*

Unfortunately I have been guilty of very great semantic sin in these letters. I have been getting further and further away from *you* in talking about *your existence.* Abstraction has obscured and lost the dear, individual person you were, and maybe are.

I want to affirm my confidence in the important reality of a kind of existence which I have not spoken of hitherto. It is not quite the same as that eternalism to which George Eliot gave a classic name when she spoke of the "choir invisible," the spirits who have flowed back into the great ocean of soul after having briefly "stained the white radiance of eternity."

What I mean is consistent with eternalism, but the eternalism of your personality as a drop in the ocean is not so important as its constant and continued individual activity in your children and friends and casual acquaintances. Their memories? Yes, of course! But your influence goes deeper than memory. Whether the cortex remembers or not,

143

the muscles and the nervous system remember. The pure and serene thoughts that possessed you during the gestation of your children are remembered; the home atmosphere during their childhood is remembered. The young women in your Ladies' Aid Society who were pleased and uplifted when you refused to gossip, and the children whom they were about to bear, remember you. The tramp who ate at your unstinted hand, sweetened by your smile and unsalted by your tongue, went away with something that stayed by him longer than the ham and eggs.

Matter is eternal. Every man, woman, and child who came within the radius of your warm, lucent eyes, your humble-proud, deprecating, heartening smile saying to each, "I don't know what trouble you're in, but you can't have been very bad; probably no worse than I, and I'm not so very bad," underwent physical changes that are still remembered. When I was eighteen my college savings went to mitigate a family catastrophe. I dared not face the ordeal of starting to college with five dollars in my pocket and thirty dollars promised. But you gave me courage. You believed in me. And I responded with a tide of resolution that has never quite subsided throughout life.

A classic we often define as a book that has lived for a century. You will be a classic November of next year, Mother. And whether you know it when the time comes, or I know it so that I may write a centennial review of the book of your life, you have made a difference in the universe.

Sawdust and Axioms

M ANY have celebrated the virtues of sawing wood, of "sawing wood and saying nothing." My opinion is that when one is sawing wood there is nothing to say. The rhythmic monotony of the saw puts the mind to sleep, and the backbreaking constancy of the effort leaves no energy for thinking. It is see-saw, see-saw, until the sibilant changes to an aspirated hee-haw, hee-haw, "and one scratches one's head sometimes to see if the hair's turned—" hide.

As for me I chop; and hanker not for a higher Olympus than a growing woodpile, nor for more ambrosial food than steaming oats and sizzling bacon after an early morning wrestle with a knotty problem in White Oak. My love for the art began when, as a youngster, I roamed the nearby hills in the Alleghenies to glean pine kindlings for the breakfast fire. To sit in the barn on rainy days and do my regular stint of splitting beautiful sections out of a perfect cylinder of golden pine was not so much work as rapture. Later, as an adolescent youth I hewed timbers along the Juniata to form the frame for a small portable mill; but when we got the saws set up, circular, and cut-off, and edger, and began to manufacture uniform boards and two-by-fours, I lost interest. The beautiful hewn hemlocks in the frame, I felt, had been put to base and unprofitable use. It might truthfully be said that I hacked my way through college, for I chopped down apple trees on the lawn of one of the professors, later chopping them up again in the woodshed. Moreover during one long blissful Christmas vacation my chum and I walked three miles daily to a tributary of the Connecticut, where we chopped and piled cordwood, chestnut and elm, discoursing the while on free will, the last Epworth League social, the coming examinations, Maude Adams, the "golden girl," and many other profound matters. In Kansas on the Kaw I chopped firewood, crooked sticks of obscure, hybrid origin whose power of pleasure is poisoned in my recollection by the heavy knot that flew off the ax stroke and broke my nose. But all these youthful operations were but apprentice work to the journeyman joy of conquering oaks, the complaisant Red and the sullen White, here in the land of the Ojibways.

I have some friends who shrug and some who frown when I babble in this strain. The shruggers I do not argue with and find it easy to forgive; they are ignorant, poor souls. Perhaps they are too far down from Neanderthal and not far enough up toward the new steel age. It may be they think I am aping the sage of Walden, the prophet of Sagamore, or the recluse of Amerongen. But after all it *was* an ax that was chiefly responsible for *Walden*.

"Near the end of March," says Thoreau, "I borrowed an axe and went down to the woods by Walden Pond, nearest to where I intended to build my house, and began to cut down some tall, arrowy white pines, still in their youth, for timber. It is difficult to begin without borrowing, but perhaps it is the most generous course thus to permit your fellowmen to have an interest in your enterprise. The owner of the axe, as he released his hold on it, said that it was the apple of his eye; but I returned it sharper than I received it." (Not unlike S. T. C., whose pencilings always enriched the margins of borrowed books.) "One day when my axe had come off and I had cut a green hickory for a wedge, driving it with a stone, and had placed the whole to soak in a pond in order to swell the wood, I saw a striped snake run into the water, and he lay on the bottom, apparently without inconvenience, as long as I stayed there, or more than a quarter of an hour; perhaps because he had not yet fairly come out of the torpid state. It appeared to me that for a like reason men remain in their present low and primitive condition; but if they should feel the influence of the spring of springs arousing them, they would of necessity rise to a higher and more ethereal life."

From which it appears that the misfortunes of an ax led to valuable discoveries. No slipped helve, no striped snake; no striped snake, no spiritual truth that day; no daily truth, no daily food for Thoreau; no daily food for Thoreau, no *Walden*, no *Week on the Concord*, no "Maine Woods," no "Excursions" for the rest of us!

The ax of Taillefer, that famous blade of Arthur (Excalibur could have been no mere scimitar), the ax of the headsman of Armentieres, of the Green Knight, and eminent among them all, Inkosikaas, the wise woodpecker of Rider Haggard's Zulu hero, Umslopogaas — all these are poets' themes that I wish my shrugging friends knew better.

Other friends there are who argue and frown. Most of them are realists. One says the energy I expend chopping a cord of wood should earn two tons of coal (all unwitting of my most valuable earnings). Another goes further and says I could sell the wood as it stands, buy kerosene with the proceeds, eliminate all the labor of chopping and the time spent in making wood fires and the excess heat on summer days and — in short, my selfish pastime is an economic horror, and I am a wastrel, though to be sure, he regards me as charitably as I do the realist of the first type, and admits that my ignorance is a partial excuse. This friend I effectively silenced once during a wet spell in June by inviting him out to the cottage for the night, and giving him his choice between a spindly, smelly kerosene stove and a solid, sweet-sour, ant-aromaed oak fire. After all, heat sensations penetrate even a pachyderm.

But another friend takes a line that is almost too much for me. I have found myself responding to him sometimes as to an hypnotic spell. He is a sociologist, somewhat tender-minded, and has made a thorough study of the Druidic religious rites. He inveigled me a while ago into reading *The Golden Bough,* after which for a season, I must admit that I wavered. I sometimes caught myself shivering as I was on the point of sinking my ax into the skin of a living tree, listening for and half expecting to hear a voice warn me in Etruscan or Erse from my profane purpose. This form of weakness I have successfully resisted however. Not by renouncing allegiance to the oak and denying kinship with my pagan and heathen ancestors; I loved and revered it and them too much for that. But I remembered that "each man kills the thing he loves," that certainly his killing it is no proof that he does not love it; and I am sure I prefer to kill mine with a sharp and merciful ax, not with such heavy, gnawing words as my friends the economists use. And so, while my dismissal of the antivivisectionist indictment is more summary than my heart feels, I cannot regard his outcry as of the first moment.

For all this there is a pang of self-accusation more painfully searching than any brought by my friends, tender- or tough-minded.

In the loving labor with seeds and plants there is something constructive, something creative. There is a solemnly beautiful joy in the assisting of Nature to produce her annual miracles, a joy that no one on this planet should be deprived of; all our fine *kultur* fails to make up to us for Eden. Sharply contrasting with this joy in assistant-creatorship is the other, perhaps savage, joy in destruction. The wood chopper, instead of lending his brain and brawn to the building processes, is rending Nature's fibers asunder, is forcing the oak, in its very etymology the symbol of strength wherever men have invented words, to selfish and unhallowed purposes. He is a demoniac vandal, brandishing his ax at Frea and Diana, with barbaric glee shearing apart

148

skeins of mysterious weaving, setting up his whim or comfort or gain before the life rights of a fellow creature.

On the other hand, I am accustomed to reflect when the ax chances to be performing well, that the vandal, the destructive critic, is not unrelated to Prometheus, who suffered for the very fire I get from the Red Oak. Prometheus was a destructive critic, as were also Lucifer and Thomas the Apostle. To build anything, something else must be destroyed. There is no exception to this law, whether in the physical or social or spiritual realms. Man is the everlasting meddler. For a house he destroys a grove, or robs the earth's crust. For a suit of clothes he disrobes a shivering animal. For a family he takes another's daughter and breaks down her life, throwing away at the same time his own. For a state he ruthlessly lops away the edges of the individual citizen in order to work out the pattern of his mosaic. For a creed he destroys another creed. For a thought he plunders books, tears asunder ideas. For a work of art he sacrifices friends and foes alike. Just as for food he katabolizes animals and plants.

A good lover, a good creator, must first be a good hater; I think God must have hated chaos. A heaven without a conflict of opinion would be a very fair imitation of hell, and Lucifer Satan in his consistent kingdom of wickedness occasionally regrets his former heady arguments with Supreme Power and swims up through chaos for some fun; just as God, according to Charles Erskine Scott Wood, sometimes remembers sentimentally the "good devil" who formerly gave heaven some piquancy. All constructive criticism of the historicity of Jesus is based upon the doubt of Thomas rather than upon the volatile enthusiasm of Peter or the inconsistent mysticism of Paul.

James Harvey Robinson has spoken of freedom as gentle and tolerant, a view which at first seems admirable and true. But as he proceeds, doubt creeps in: "There is a French proverb that to understand is to forgive. But one can go further and say that to understand is to see that there is nothing to forgive." This carries us into the realm of sweet thought with a vengeance. May there be a point where tolerance ceases to be a virtue? Robinson thought not, and he was right if all things are alike good. But I cannot believe that Jesus of Nazareth and Abraham Lincoln, whom I somehow bracket together, would have agreed with him. The first tolerated many kinds of sins and sinners: a tax farmer, a woman taken in adultery, winebibbers and bandits; but he did not try to conceal his scorn of Pharisaism and his wrath at sacrilege. The other found it easy to pardon war crimes considered punishable by shooting, not only the pathetic crimes of overstrained boys who slept at their posts, but even adult technical traitors, for his great heart knew the rents torn by war psychology. Still he hated common liars and men that ground the faces of the poor and those that preyed upon the bleeding body of their prostrate country.

These were both men of liberal views, but each had a cutting word for certain kinds of unrighteousness. The reasonable theft, even the casual murder, may readily find sanctuary in a liberal mind; but the agents of White Slavery, the traders and politicians who deliberately debauch a nation with opium or imperialism, the professional servants of God whose chief concern is soft food and raiment and pews that worship the pulpit — these must be met by something else than gentleness and tolerance. The perfect liberal may be perfectly limber; if so, I must hold that there is a point where limberness ceases to be virtue. My ax is never tolerant when the question of hurting the feelings of some parasite is involved.

The ax sings a various tune, different with the droning accompaniment of July mud daubers from that of its staccato

solo in late November. Sometimes when the stick is of
waved and wrinkled texture, not so much in knots as bound
together by many tough and interlocked fingers of fiber
dead many a year but still firm set, the bit bites deep and
holds. Then there is work for stout heart and sinewy triceps.
With the relief given by a small ax wedge, sunk accurately
from the other end of the billet, I wrench my big ax free
and smite deep and straight into the cleft. Sullenly, almost
passively the wood accepts the challenge. The slowly acquired strength of a century is no light thing to yield at a
blow or be frightened at a threat. Here is one of Nature's
conservatives, which the radical ax will find hard to convert.

Conservatives are of at least two types: complete and incomplete. Nothing makes an indelible impression in water;
to write words there is like reasoning with a mystic, like appealing to the imagination of an oyster. The Red Sea parts
but rushes together again and that convenient ford is irre-
trievably lost. "One cannot hold soft cheese with a hook,"
said old Epictetus, thinking of the minds of certain of his
disciples. Nevertheless even the softest cheese may be dipped up in a sieve that the liquid mind runs through, placid
and forgiving. The cheese mind, exasperating as it is, does
not madden the curious prospector completely, for his pan
retains now and then a stringy coating. The mind that does
not even leave the sieve damp is your perfect conservative.

The oak fibers are not so complete in their conservatism
as some of their cousin reactionaries; the oak is more open
to reason, and the incisive stroke of the ax, applied again
and again in the same fissure, finally starts a process of re-
consideration. The little fiber minds have been so long co-
herent in a tangle of prejudices that they naturally believe
their order the order of Nature, their ideas the only proper
ideas. Now they are jolted; they still have enough life to
change their minds — and they do it, with infinitesimal
speed at first, a bit sullenly, but at the end with a frank,

151

wide-open grin. So does the mind of a youth here and there miraculously crack wide open and rejoice the heart of his teacher, for the phenomenon does not occur often within his ken; and he knows there is more joy in heaven over one pattern-broken mind than over ninety and nine wise persons who need but will have no redistribution of their neurons. Especially does heaven make jolly over the youthful radical and grieve for the congenital middle-aged. The physical optics of youth are inclined to nearsightedness, but his ideal vision is always hyperopic — indicating a wise provision for the sad, inevitable contraction later on.

Like the British Parliament and even the United States Senate, the oak stump has its radical members. Dealings with them must become truly *axio-mattock*, for the grubbing hoe must join issue with the revolutionary ax in order to probe deeply enough into the affair. When grub meets hoe, then comes the tug o' war. Interlocking directorates have nothing on the intricate stubbornness of the consolidated roots of an oak, starting out honestly as if to spread in the ordinary way, then out of sight turning inward and reaching down to Auvernus in the form of a tap. No victory is better earned than this of following some Alcestis, Hercules-fashion, to the depths, and wrenching her from the very jaws of Hades.

The saw has no liberal nor liberating effect. It leaves the complex of prejudice as tangled and impervious on both sides of the cut as it was before. The sawdust serves no purpose but to blind the eyes of the sawyer, who imagines that his arbitrary, cross-grain tactics are changing the mind of the oak. His reform leaves the inside of the proselyte unchanged, for the saw has used irrational, dictatorial methods, and with the incomplete conservative, this approach neither enlightens nor moves. A little grain of sawdust here, a little grain of sawdust there — and finally there are two stubborn, unyielding billets where there was one twice their length before, but neither is one whit more usable in my restricted firebox. The reasonable ax now appeals to their whole longitudinal being, and once convinced of my zealous integrity of purpose they yield with a gratifying wholeheartedness.

If heaven provides some weeks for berry picking in July and August, or that segment of eternity corresponding, I shall be well pleased. But there must certainly be some wood chopping. And that may seem as gratuitous a pursuit in heaven as (with reverse English) carrying coals to Newcastle. But since there must surely be eternity for reading and talk with friends — not Big Talk, nor Small Talk, but genuine, radical, longitudinal talk like the long pursuing fiber of the oak, there must be an open fire. If I get a chance to discover my mistake in this hope, I shall want to emigrate.

God,

I shall side in with Noyes,

> *this is hell; not heaven;*
> *Give me the fire and a friend or two.*

The Oak (with variations)

The Oak-folk are up throughout the state,
They're going great.
Their pennons flame in maroon and gold;
They whip in the wind but mean to hold
Over the winter.

But Oak-folk comply to a humble fate;
They go to the grate.
Their sinews snap with purpose bold,
Their tongues out-thrust to dare the cold
Of the winter.

. . . .

Now what has become of the Scarlet Oak?
He's up in smoke.
But his ghost resides in the ant-y smells,
In the oldsters' smiles and the children's yells;
His ghost revives in the reveries,
In the gleeful gab and the cheerful jibe,
In the tale, the song, and the diatribe.

The ghost of the Oak is now a joke,
Is now a tender, purling cloak
To a lover's allegory —
Or it is now a curling smoke
Over a tale of glory —
Or the final stroke to a bedtime story.
    One thing you never will find the Oaks
    Supporting, and that is hoax.
    Nor will it revoke, the Oak.

154

Oh the oaks, burr, scarlet and white and red,
And tough with the toughness of what I said,
(Not gray with the grayness of aught that's dead)
They stand with burly Swede stolidity —
Not much harmed by the scant humidity.
They stand with a stubborn English grace,
With dug-in toes, and a poker face.
They stand with a careless Yankee ease,
With a damficare and a gosyouplease.
They stand by ones and twos and threes
They stand up straight or on crooked knees.
They stand alone or hand clasped in hand.
   The southern bretheren stand in the lake,
   The northern stand on the land.
   But the point they make is that of Saint Paul,
   For having done all, they stand.

     · · · · · · · · · · · · ·

Oak's tender, green, and graceful leaves that all
The summer long accepted loan of root
And rain, to spread a panorama, and
Inspire the Oak to noble growth,
Are not content with this achievement.
When November shrills and warns the woods to shelter,
The bold male leaves start rustling back defiance,
Proclaiming they will take their chance on bough —
Prevail on Nature's law, prolong their loan
To live another year.
                  The female kind
Float softly down to earth, consoled to feel
That nestling acorns need their covering warmth;
While certain generous mother chromosomes
Remember pretty, shy, young flowerets
That winked back daily at them from beneath
And bore no foliage to guard their seed.

So down they croon to knit a coverlet
For phlox, blue gentian, and anemone.

The cottager whose home's embosomed in
A sheet of tinder, plies his ruthless rake.
And Spring's new-running sap will shake and loose
The stubborn grip of those who loved their lives
Not wisely nor in season.

November 1935

My Father's Bayonet

THE bare, white, ascetic walls of my student's cell are shocked by few ornaments. In the center of a great blank, above fifteen feet of friendly books, and looking fondly down on the back of my head as the original used to look years ago when her young Ulysses was struggling in the coils of two Unknown Quantities, either of which was insidious enough and mean enough to enthrall him, hangs the picture of a sweet-faced woman. Her hair has a suspicion of silver and her lips the hint of a smile. On the table before me, in the midst of an orderly chaos, unanswered letters, writing pads, Shakespeare, *The Deeds of Beowulf, The Japanese Three Graces,* and all the paraphernalia of the pedant and the sedent — right in the moil of work, where she belongs, sits a little decisive Scotch head framed in a square of gold. The eyes — wonderful eyes, with spots of red like the speckled mountain trout of the Alleghenies — rest on me always. In their aura of love I catch a flash of fun, a veil of reproach, a mist of compassion. Besides these two attendants and the books which flank and hedge me about, the only noteworthy companion of my solitude dangles from the top of the brown walnut dresser — my father's bayonet! There it hangs — a trumpet of the Sixties. No profane hand has ever offended by polishing the rusty steel or furbishing the copper belt plate. No attempt has been made to bring it into harmony with the new age. It has never been fraternized. Its message is as stern and uneuphemistic as in '65. The very sweat of the Wilderness still whitens the leather belt. The scars on the scabbard spell Cold Harbor and Spottsylvania as indubitably as they did

NOTE. First published in the *Methodist Review*, January 1909.

157

forty years before Brander Matthews, and now, as I look at
it for the thousandth time, my father's account of how it
came into his possession creeps back out of boyhood recollections.

The Army of the Potomac had camped for the night in an
auspicious vicinity and early in the morning "while it was
yet night," my progenitor, then seventeen years old and un-
surfeited by chickory and hardtack, began a series of com-
missary investigations at an outlying farm. Satisfied with the
fine ham and yams, my father, who was a connoisseur of
millinery as well as of gastronomies, had climbed in an upper window (the inmates had all fled) to refresh himself
with the sight of at least the *shell* of a woman. Foolishly,
and unsoldierly, he left his gun below on the stoop. Only a
minute and he was aroused from his soft revel in hoops and
flounces by a yell from a passing soldier, and, looking out
of the window, saw his regiment moving off. He slid hastily
down a post and to his consternation found his gun — gone.
(There must be Irish somewhere in the ancestry.) It was no
time for vain regret and he started on the triple-quick after
his regiment. Fortune favored him. His course lay past a
persimmon tree with a soldier at the top and a gun at the
bottom. Father grabbed the gun without breaking step and
was soon lost in the moving column. The poor fellow who
was treed kept yelling futilely in his chagrin: "Drop that
gun, you son of a gun." I have since doubted if the soldier
may not have assigned some other pedigree to the cheerful
robber, because the repetition of the word "gun" in so short
a sentence is rhetorically weak; but father was usually vera-
cious and I repeat his exact words. Thus the bayonet came
into the family — typical of plunder.

War must ever be lawless. It may be undertaken in order
to enforce law, but it is in its nature and methods lawless.
So must every change be. Inertia is the only condition con-
formable to the past — the one purely law-abiding attitude.

Revolution and progress must be anarchic. You must have war if you would not have death. When you no longer hear the clash of principles be sure Beelzebub is lord and has bribed or gagged the voices of righteousness. There was war in the old heaven and there will be war in the new heaven, else it will not be worth inhabiting. A company where with one accord all are good would soon find it out, admit it, and tell each other about it — and then there would be the devil to pay. I do not prefer Lucifer and Moloch to Michael and Gabriel, but I do believe they will always be on deck and worthy of hostile steel. Voltaire it was who said: "If God did not exist, man would do well to invent him." I am inclined to think that if there is no devil, and some have hinted it darkly, man should make one for a spiritual buffer. He ought to be just "a stuff to try the soul's strength on." I do not advocate any more devils, because, even if Satan himself has gone, he has left a numerous progeny of imps who are able to squeeze into smaller corners of the soul hearth than their heroic father ever noticed. With the heightened complexions and increased complexities of society, temptations to hoodwink plain old Morality and suck the egg without a scratch on the shell, have become legion, and just in proportion has developed diabolical skill in performing. But man is spared the necessity of inventing Satan just because these little imps have remained. We do not need to go abroad to tilt; in our own rooms we may find enough exercise of this sort.

The bayonet has not been left so far behind. This relic not only reminds me of heroic struggles of a past age; it tells me I too must fight. It says life is hard; it warns me that ease invites sloth and sloth breeds death. Maybe it is because I am so "incurably Protestant," that my blood has been so charged with the "dissidence of dissent and the Protestantism of the Protestant religion," that I see a serpent behind so many roses of beauty and enjoyment; anyway, I think the bayonet speaks sooth. It has become a recent fashion to deride the old figure of the Christian life as a battle. It ought to be a triumphal procession with brass band and frequent stops for red lemonade and ice cream cones, from the moment the "soul is saved"—as if ever a soul was "saved" for good and all by a single prayer or a single act of repentance. Well, I remember what Christ said, "Not peace, but a sword." Life was not easy for Him. To the best of earth this has been no parade ground, but a battle-field. Be suspicious of the offer of serenity in this life. You may be getting mere spiritual morphine. The man who lays down his arms and lets somebody else or something else—some God or some church—fight for him, the while he reposes in irresponsible comatoseness, has not won the fight but has deserted the cause and forfeited his hope of everlasting reward.

"Oh," I hear, "but you are making the good life unhappy and discouraging people from following it." Good! They ought to be scared away that follow for the loaves and fishes. Survival of the fittest reigns in the spiritual world, too. Happiness? What's happiness? Did anybody ever die to win happiness? If so, I wonder if he found it. The man who loses his life in saving another's because of the pleasure he has in doing good—well, that man is looking inward and he had better *look out*!

"But you make yourself actually unhappy by your continual ferment of conviction."

Be it so. I would rather grow tired than be always *ennuyé*; I would rather have the idea of something better that I do not have, and be unhappy for the want of it, than be contented with the lower thing that comes if we merely keep step and follow safe leaders.

Then may the sweat of forced marches and the blood of battle remain on the old bayonet! There is no time to make clean and pretty. After polishing our faith and scouring our religion we might fear to tamper with life because of the taint of skepticism so apt to strike in, and so draw them from their sheaths only in the sanctity of the church and surrounded by the brethren. I prefer to let the microbes do their worst on the steel of the sword of the spirit. They cannot injure it.

CHRISTMAS, 1906

When lovers are apart, dear heart—
What foolish word was that?
How can true lovers be apart?
Who can divide the one in heart?
What should I say, I wonder,
When lovers are asunder?
What then make they
Of Christmas Day,
Is it so poor as some men say?
Ah no, dear love, not so.

For then, each time a letter brings
A living breath,
A joyful voice of Christmas sings
Of love and God and power over death.
Christ is born
On every morn.
Lovers like us,
Though sundered far
Have one eternal Bethlehem star;
And lovers like us,
I say, alway
Have one perpetual Christmas Day.

Two Bites at a Poem

Singed moth never fears the flame,
That is, till he's singed enough.
Mold of life runs still the same,
Singed moth never fears the flame:
This is such a jolly game
For a moth who's wise and tough.
Singed moth never fears the flame
Till he's really singed enough.

Deep-slung in a cradle of mother earth
Snuggle the oaklet leaves to burn;
Close to the womb that knew their birth
Fair-play death will have his turn.

Rake them in and let them burn;
No fear, their playmate breeze is gone.
Desiccate bodies writhe and turn
For a magic rug to rise upon.

Now I can let them safely yearn
Far from the deep-piled ranks of friends;
Now I can loll, perhaps discern
The metaphysic of means and ends.

Rustle, lift, hiss, spire . . .
Quick, the mop! Will I never learn?
The breeze is back, the wood's afire!
Fair-play death will have his turn.

April 27, 1941

On Some Uses of Audacity

NONE of the many stories related of John Paul Jones, authentic and questionable, has a more inevitable moral or a more happy veraciousness than that of his reputed reply to a superior's caution, "Remember that discretion is the better part of valor." "Very well," said John Paul, "but damned impudence is the better part of discretion."

Impudence, or rather audacity, is one of the glorious virtues of youth; the supreme tragedy of middle age is the gradual loss of it and the substitution of discretion — "judgment"— as some middle-aged persons whose enthusiasms and feet have grown cool prefer to call it. In reality it is neither the one nor the other, but a tremulous premonition, advance agent of senility. For there is no essential contradiction between judgment and audacity. The best, most living and athletic judgment must have its quota of audacity, without which it is but an emasculated reminiscence. "Fools rush in where angels fear to tread" is the question-begging wisdom of middle age, for if it is true, there are no young angels and no old fools. "There's method in his madness" similarly is a grudging admission that strangeness and difference may be compatible with sanity.

There are three ways of playing at games of chance: first, to sit pat and play the bird in the hand; second, to throw judgment to the winds and plunge blindly with a prayer; third, to compute all the elements of chance in the situation, and behind the poker face await with serenity the outcome of an impudent judgment, cashing in immediately on a success or later on the experience gained by failure.

NOTE. First published in the *Hamline Review*, June 1921.

It is not a matter of years, this middle age. The plasticity of the brain cortex and the pliability of the arteries determines it, though occasionally it forestalls these physical postulates and attains reality through the spirit alone, when a dash of audacity has been omitted. I once knew a man whose face had been born forty years before his body, and it is no secret that there are gray-heads on our faculties whose minds are younger than those of many of their undergraduate disciples. For middle age, like Boston, is a state of mind. Conventional people, who conform themselves to this world, if not born in middle age, achieve it by the sophomore year and exchange it only for the "lean and slippered pantaloon" of senescence. They do not like to take a chance; they do not want to live dangerously, but desire of college that it should teach them what the world has rewarded and how best to shape themselves to its present requirements.

For the literary neophyte who studies the art of self-expression, there are many major commandments: Unity, Coherence, Emphasis, Mass, Proportion; or Clearness, Accuracy, Beauty, Force; these with Sincerity comprise an authoritative decalogue. But without Audacity these make only tame and proper spinners — and spinsters — of words. These are of the form, formal. Without audacity of sentiment or thought they have nothing about them wild and free.

It is a mistake to suppose that social pertness and verbal audacity are usually found in the same people. True, Benevenuto Cellini, the swashbuckling egotist and artist of the early sixteenth century, has a goodly measure of literary "punch," but compared with his mild and urbane contemporary, the French country lawyer, Montaigne, he is as tame as a house cat. In truth a salty style but ill comports with a "fresh" manner of talk, as many a pert miss in college has had the occasion though probably not the grace to learn. Neither does a peppery disposition express itself often in salty discourse; it is too volatile and not sufficiently sedimentary. Only the careful writer can be audacious, for no other realizes the possibilities of the edged tools with which he works.

Although all great writers must deal dangerously with their material, it is among the essayists and letter-writers that this art reaches perfection, those whose chief aim is personal revelation. From the dialogues of Plato, the letters of Paul, the prefaces of Saxon Alfred, and the *Essais* of Montaigne effervesces a stream of salt augmented and strengthened by a score of later fountains. When an oldster retains his audacity the angels rejoice (as they did when the venerable Jowett remarked to Margot Tennant, "We must keep our faith in God despite what the clergy tell us"), though when he loses it they are not much surprised. But their tears flow freely when a youngster cheats himself by putting on an early middle age. This is indubitable tragedy, that the flight of time should be artificially accelerated.

Liberation of the mind from the trammels of every kind of prejudice is the ideal of a college education. Possibly there should be a college entrance examination in openmindedness, and those who show a stubborn conservatism at the age of eighteen should be rejected as unfit. They can be only a drag on the progress of the world and might better be put to work where their inert minds can do little harm. For youth has an indubitable obligation to be radical; in no other way can it escape the tragedy of middle-age reaction and death. Or if this policy of exclusion seems too harsh on congenital middle age, we might establish a chair of Audacity, and require a year's credit of all candidates for a *liberal* arts degree.

Again April

And that was April too,
When lilacs bloomed in the door-yard,
A terribly sweet, a terribly final time,
A time for love and the beginning of immortality.

Now the red-bud blooms on the hills of Georgia
As our friend — *Greater love hath no man than this,*
That a man lay down his life for his friends —
Bids the red-bud goodby, and North to the Hudson,
As American a river as the Sangamon,
The funeral cortege passes.

And April was the time of the great master of them both,
A terribly sweet, a terribly final time,
A sacrificial beginning time
For love, brother-love, courage,
And the beginning of immortality.
Nothing to fear but fear, said one;
Don't be troubled; I guess we shall get through, the
    other.

Time for re-birth of their courage, and the Four Freedoms.
Time of that other freedom, for him
In "the sure enwinding arms of cool-enfolding death,"
The final freedom in the return of those borrowed for
    great tasks,
Who have worthily fulfilled them.

A time of consecration
For those who remain,
Through many a dark, to a distant golden April.

April 15, 1945

Abraham Lincoln – Man of Letters

THAT Abraham Lincoln is the most and best beloved man of the nineteenth century will not, I surmise, be seriously questioned. During his lifetime some there were who hated him, because they feared and had reason to fear honesty. Many there were who ridiculed him for his birth, his breeding, his ungainliness, his uncouthness, even for his boyish vanity in altitude. He wrote to Hackett, the actor, "I have endured a great deal of ridicule without much malice; and have received a great deal of kindness not quite free from ridicule. I am used to it."

At a dinner in St. Paul not long ago, I was perhaps extravagantly shocked to discover an intelligent woman who could speak slightingly of "poor Lincoln," with the implication that he did the best he could but had made a sad failure. There are not many like her, however, North or South. Most of those who sat in the seat of the scornful came to agree with that cold, logic-chopping John Stuart Mill when he wrote soon after the assassination that Lincoln "had gradually won, not only the admiration, but almost the personal affection of all who love freedom or appreciate simplicity or uprightness." The "almost" has disappeared. In a volume entitled *Abraham Lincoln: The Tribute of the Synagogue,* edited by Rabbi Emanuel Hertz, there are many beautiful tributes that might seem excessive were it not for their almost uniform high dignity and sincerity. One speaker said that Lincoln had no ancestry, no fellows, no successors, that he approximated the genius of the Hebrew people and presented a close parallel to Hillel, the wood chopper of Palestine. Another said, "He has proved himself the suffering Messiah, the Vicarious Atonement";

167

while a third suggested using the blank pages that separate the Old from the New Testament for the life and achievements of Lincoln, "a chapter of sacred history . . . God bless his name." Yes, he is beloved.

Four etchings appeared in the photogravure section of the *St. Paul Pioneer Press* on February 14, 1937, taken from the Lincoln Museum at Fort Wayne. The artists were of four different nationalities: an American, a German, an English Jew, and a Swede. Each artist had created Lincoln in his own racial image; in the etching by the German, Lincoln was German, by the Hebrew, Hebrew, by the Swede, Swedish. This remarkable alchemy was so striking as to be slightly ludicrous, saved however by the worshipful, illumined spirit.

No man has ever endured the scrutiny of more searching eyes. First, the political muckrakers, who sift the ordure in the back yard of every president; then the idol-worshippers; finally the historical students, patiently and pitilessly exhuming every bone of fact and dusting it with the softest feather to preserve its contours. In 1906 Daniel Fish published a Lincoln bibliography containing 1080 items; in 1925 J. B. Oakleaf added 1600 more, making a total of nearly 2700. Since then there has been a steadily increasing stream, headed by Carl Sandburg's two-volume prose fantasy, *The Prairie Years*, his four volumes on *The War Years*, the late Senator Beveridge's projected three-volume work of political analysis, only two volumes of which were finished, and the yearly augmented work of the assiduous late-lamented Barton. There are now in existence close to 4000 books and separately published brochures concerned directly and primarily with Lincoln's life and personality. Today in Fort Wayne the Lincoln Foundation Library contains 7500 volumes including translations, hundreds of bound magazine articles, and more hundreds of prints.

It would be difficult to prove that this enormous bibliography is justified by the historic importance of the subject. Certainly I should not attempt either to prove or disprove that Lincoln's is the most important in the history of the nineteenth century. This library has been compiled by good, bad, and indifferent writers, scholars, pseudo scholars, journalists, and amateurs, because the subject interested them. Because Lincoln is beloved!

Why was he so beloved? Rather, why *is* he so beloved?

Certainly not because he was an excellent lawyer of thoroughly proved integrity! Just as surely not because he was an astute and skillful politician, although the Republican party has particular reason for devoutly thanking God for such a founder. (I do not mean to imply that the present GOP is what he founded.) Was he beloved as the emancipator of four millions of men and women, as one who set the Negro free, in the trite phrase, "with the stroke of a pen"? Well yes, a stroke of the pen set them free — on paper. Emancipation, though a spectacular concomitant of the man and the time, is a frail claim upon the gratitude of posterity, leaving as it did all the serious problems of racial prejudice still to deal with. His death prevented the full deliverance he hoped for, and perhaps even his genius might have proved unequal to the immensities and complexities of the ensuing tragedy. In a Sunday supplement article a few years ago, the view was advanced that Lincoln was luckier than many famous figures who outlived their fame. "It is apparent to the most hasty reader," said the pundit, "first, that Lincoln died at just the right time; second, that Grant should have died when Lincoln died." I do not agree in this cliché of popular criticism. Note the exact words: "It is apparent to the most hasty reader . . ." This is an example of subconscious control with the result that the author wrote better than he knew. It is apparent perhaps to the *most hasty* reader, but not to the less hasty or to the ordinarily good reader. The author reasoned that since Grant was duped by the political reptiles that flourished in the post-bellum swamps and ended in official fiasco, so Lincoln would have been duped by the same meretricious lies and liars. This is a gross fallacy, an egregious example of non sequitur. The syndicator says that Lincoln's greatness came to him late in life. I deny it. Every reader of Sandburg's *Prairie Years* recognizes the slow, steady, persistent growth of Lincoln's moral and intellectual stature. A man may gain reputation after the age of fifty, but he does not "become great."

A learned historian in another popular essay tepidly supports the charge that Lincoln and Republican leaders could have avoided the "immeasurable catastrophes of Civil War and Reconstruction" if he had not held to his "house divided against itself" speech of 1858, made before he had become "great," and they had been willing to support the Crittenden Compromise in December 1860.* Aside from his fondness for compromise, the author is guilty of two major blunders: first, he ignores the fact that Lincoln repeatedly had urged "compensated emancipation," surely the most enlightened practical method of obtaining the wished-for results of "compromise" without the stultification of principles inherent in the Crittenden Compromise; and second, had Lincoln lived to complete his second term, Reconstruction would have borne no resemblance to what it was under Stanton, Johnson, and Grant.

This has been a not irrelevant digression.

Is Lincoln beloved because he was a great war president? In this respect perhaps his claims are weakest. Many of his generals thought him a meddler; even though his interference was often justified by results, it sometimes contributed to the vacillations of vacillators. His magnanimity and all his human passions did not invariably produce an efficient

* Henry W. Lawrence in the *Universal Weekly*, February 12, 1939.

war president, who must be ruthless. Besides, all wars pass, and history is writing them smaller and smaller. What atomic wars may achieve is in the lap of the future. The probability is that World War III will leave no history, because no historian.

As upholder of the Union? Undoubtedly this was his task, in his own conception. Still even here there may be intelligent difference in evaluation. Certainly this work as such cannot explain his universal appeal to the world's heart.

As symbol and regenerator of democracy? In the final eloquent chapter of one of the latest and most remarkable studies of Lincoln, a critical digest of his most important biographers, the author, after noting that each man or woman, though limited by personal bias, had discovered a part of the truth and contributed to the portrait for posterity, had this to say:

"Earlier Lincoln books — those written during his presidency or shortly afterwards — tended to stress the poverty to fame motif. Then came the theme of the Great Emancipator, followed by that of the saviour of the Union. After the turn of the century, with these themes about worked out, Lincoln literature became spotty and static until World War I brought challenge to Democracy and its ideals.

"For a long time Lincoln had been regarded as the prime example of the opportunities that Democracy affords the ordinary man, but now he began to be viewed, not only in this light, but also as the most powerful personal force behind the democratic movement."*

This is the widest, most significant claim thus far noted. But we must keep in mind that World War II again put democracy to the stretch, brought forward new heroes better adapted to the particular problems, and today the victory is still in the balance. Could Lincoln have been granted even half of Bernard Shaw's third of Methuselah's life span, and

*Benjamin P. Thomas in *Portrait for Posterity*.

171

could he have continued to grow as he did during his short fifty years, he might conceivably have worked out the answer and been able to *demonstrate* the ultimacy of the democratic ideal.

Why is a man beloved? Personality! What is the secret of greatness? Character! Sometimes in rare and happy instances, the answer is the same. Personality and character are connected with a man's passional life. Lincoln's passions were for learning through reading and listening, and for communication through speaking and writing. I genuinely believe and wish here to maintain that Lincoln's word magic is at every stage inseparable from his career and that Lincoln the man of letters will live longer than Lincoln the emancipator or the upholder of the Union, or even the avatar of democracy.

According to Billy Herndon, when 22-year-old Abe Lincoln turned up at New Salem on election day, 1831, looking for his would-be employer, Denton Offutt, and was pressed into service as a clerk because he "reckoned he could make some hen-tracks," it was one of the stories he told to entertain the entire male community assembled that gave him entree into their admiring regard. That was the famous yarn about the little lizard and the pioneer Baptist preacher with the one-gallus trousers and the indignant lady who arose in her place and scorched the fat preacher whom the active little lizard had reduced to garments less than Johannine with "Well, if *you* are the representative of Christ, I'll never read the Bible again." This story serves as a true portrait of the lusty, gusty young giant from Goose Neck Prairie on that August day and, properly interpreted, explains his power over men. (I say "men" advisedly, for he was a man's man. Lincoln did not know the art to read "the mind's construction in the face" of women; in his letters and direct incidences with women, he was stupid to a degree; as Stephen

172

Vincent Benet wrote on one of his inspired pages, he had only patience and that was not enough.) If Lincoln had been a mere purveyor of other men's yarns — as he modestly averred on one occasion — this trait would have explained nothing significant in his career. But if, as I think can be shown, Lincoln was a creator, a *fabulist*, this story-telling power helped to create his career.

Let us go back a way — back to those years in Gentryville, Indiana, which have been so dark until recently* and still remain not fully explored, and ask what exactly fed his mind while his body was growing long and sinewy on bacon and corn pone.

What books if any were in the various homes of Thomas Lincoln during the life of Abraham's mother, Nancy, we do not surely know. But when Sarah Bush Johnston came with her three children and two fine feather beds and whatnot in December 1818 to care for the forlorn children, Sarah and Abe, left motherless by the "milk-sick" the winter before, the most important part of her cargo was a tiny, unusual frontier library. There was *Robinson Crusoe, Pilgrim's Progress, Sindbad the Sailor,* and *Aesop's Fables.* All allegory and simple narrative! Abe was going on eleven. There is strong evidence that he read and reread all of these, probably committed many passages to memory. Then why, one may naturally ask, if Lincoln was a purveyor of other men's stories, why do we not get more direct echoes from this early reading? I have kept this question hovering over my reading of his complete writings, and I feel fairly confident that not one of the twelve volumes of Nicolay and Hay, nor the million and a quarter words that Sandburg emptied from his bottomless notebooks reveal Lincoln rehearsing a fable from Aesop *in toto,* or even in complete *esse.* He seems to have formed the early habit of creative

*Tarbell and Barton have turned the spotlight on Kentucky, but it was reserved for Beveridge to uncover some significant facts about those important years, from seven to twenty-one, in Indiana.

reading and translated his classic originals into prairie set-
tings by a spontaneous leap of imagination.

There was, of course, the Bible. His mother — it rings
false to this good woman's insight and devotion to call her
stepmother — his mother said in later years that Abe was no
great reader of the Bible, but I surmise her memory was at
fault. Either then or later he must have drunk deep at the
font of King James.

He had Grimshaw's *History of the United States,* a strongly antislavery text. He had Bailey's *Etymological Dictionary*
(1725) bought by Levi Hall, who married the mother of
Dennis Hanks. This was an extraordinary book to have been
carried to a pioneer community. It is tempting to say that
it was the most important book of all in Lincoln's development. No man since Socrates had a more living passion for
accuracy in definition, while his frontier realism helped him
to a semantic interpretation far beyond Socrates. The only
thing that ever irritated Abe, according to Dennis Hanks,
was the fuzzy use of big words by some itinerant preacher
or stumping politician. Lincoln himself told J. P. Gulliver
years later that he often lay awake nights trying to put
things he heard into better, simpler words. In Dennis' picturesque phrase Abe "would mull over everything in sight,
scent and hearing . . . and wear them slick, greasy, and
threadbare."

He had Weems's *Life of Washington and of Franklin.* This
was the book borrowed from Josiah Crawford that got wet
and gave rise to the idyllic story that Lincoln offered to
work out the damages. The truth seems to be that Crawford
demanded payment in work; the boy rather sulkily pulled
corn two or three days and then composed a lampoon on
Crawford to complete payment.

He had the *Kentucky Perceptor* by an unknown compiler
and Quinn's *Jests,* popularly known as the King's Jester,
which he used to read to the boys but was never known to

quote directly in his later parables. He had the revised statutes of Indiana, the property of David Turnham; these he read with the same catholic interest he bestowed upon Aesop.

Not until later did he discover Euclid's *Elements of Geometry*, which he studied on sleepless nights on his expansive itinerary of the eighth judicial district of Illinois. In 1860, replying to a question concerning his education, he said to Mr. J. P. Gulliver:

"In the course of my law reading I constantly came upon the word *demonstrate*. I thought at first that I understood its meaning, but soon became satisfied that I did not. [How many human beings become satisfied when they discover their ignorance at a point of presumed knowledge? Yet satisfaction at the discovery of ignorance while it can still be remedied is an absolute requirement for honest scholarship.] I said to myself, 'What do I mean when I demonstrate more than when I reason or prove? How does demonstration differ from any other proof?' I consulted Webster's dictionary. That told of certain proof, proof beyond a doubt; but I could form no idea of what sort of proof that was. . . . I consulted all the dictionaries and books of reference I could find, but with no better results. You might as well have defined blue to a blind man. At last I said 'Lincoln, you can never make a lawyer if you do not understand what demonstrate means,' and I left my situation in Springfield, went home to my father's house, and stayed there till I could give any proposition in the six books of Euclid at sight. I then found out what demonstrate means, and went back to my law studies."

It was later, under the tutelage of Jack Kelso, the town drunkard, that he discovered Shakespeare; it was in the famous grab bag bought for fifty cents from a needy mover that he found Blackstone's *Commentaries*, and it was from John C. Calhoun that he borrowed the treatise on the *The-*

ory and Practice of Surveying. This, with the devoted help of the schoolmaster, Mentor Graham, he thoroughly mastered in six weeks' spare time, an intellectual feat that entitles him to a high IQ rating.

Three other books which Lincoln surely read, according to Beveridge, are Scott's *Lessons in Elocution,* Kirkham's *An Essay on Elocution,* and Newman's *Practical System of Rhetoric.* This book is still in existence, inscribed with Lincoln's name and with copious annotations. He drew bold lines across the top and down the sides of this paragraph:

"A good style is an attainment which amply repays all the effort that has here been enjoined. It is to the scholar a consummation of his intellectual discipline and acquirements. He who in this land of free institutions holds an able pen, has a weapon of powerful efficacy both for defence and attack; and if this weapon be wielded with honest and patriotic motives, he who wields it may become a public benefactor."

A marginal notation reads, "A truth very well constructed. A. L." (Euclid was still running strong in him.) Lincoln engraved the essence of this paragraph on the tablets of his mind and molded his life's activities with an absolute devotion to its precepts. (Happy the textbook writer who can achieve one such result!)

These were the books that more or less shaped Lincoln's fine mind in his early years. He did not know *Gulliver's Travels,* apparently, nor did he even know the name of Swift, a fact passing strange because of the Swiftian character of some of his early lampoons such as the famous "Rebecca" letter — which, to make the analogy complete, has the same theme as the *Drapier's Letters,* a debased currency — and his implicit theory of style, which was identical with Swift's, "proper words in proper places."

Of his later reading there is surprisingly little authentic documentation. His Springfield law partner, Herndon, whose whole life was devoted to the collection of documentary facts, reminiscences of his idol, and searching his memory to aid every biographer who applied to him until his death in 1891, was himself a wide reader and had collected an excellent library. Lincoln's reading in the law was wide, deep, and thorough; but Herndon, who in spite of much vilification by pietists and romanticists had a passion for truth-telling, says Lincoln never read a book through (he once started *Ivanhoe* but did not finish it): "Beyond a limited acquaintance with Shakespeare, Byron and Burns, Mr. Lincoln, comparatively speaking, had no knowledge of literature." Herndon was limited in poetry and did not realize how frequently and fully Lincoln's soul was immersed in the few poets he knew.

Let us now glance at Lincoln's first compositions during the green years.

Abe was the best speller, the best penman, and the best reciter in the Gentryville school. He composed several pieces of verse which have been preserved, and no doubt many that mercifully have not. Nevertheless it is easy to ridicule his verses unjustly. There are some fine lines in those which he wrote in 1844 on revisiting his Indiana home; one line, I think, has in it the touch of poetic magic:

> *The friends I left that parting day,*
> *How changed as time has sped!*
> *Young childhood grown, strong manhood gray;*
> AND HALF OF ALL ARE DEAD.

Change "of all" to "of them" and there is little pathos, no hovering accent, no magic.

In 1826 Abe's sister, Sarah, was married to Aaron Grigsby. The wedding song which he composed for the occasion, the only example of his early pieces that has come down to us, was probably the most pretentious. Some doubt has been thrown upon Lincoln's originality in this pint-sized story of creation, a similar thing by one William Bozarth having been discovered in the original manuscript, dated 1818. At all events, Abe considerably improved his original, in which process he has had plenty of respectable literary forebears. The last stanza of the ballad goes neatly this way:

> *The woman she was taken*
> *From under Adam's arm,*
> *So she must be protected*
> *From injuries and harm.*

A feud grew up between the Grigsbys and young Abe. Two of the brothers, Reuben and Charles, were married on the same day, and Abe was not invited to the merrymaking. He composed a piece of mock-Biblical writing of the genre once so popular entitled "The Chronicles of Reuben." Its success was sweet ointment to the wounded young buck who was just beginning to feel his literary oats. Its local and temporary success was due to the Chaucerian flavor of the main incident, the exchange of the brides; but to us the pith of one or two phrases gives it interest. "It came to pass when the sons of Reuben grew up that they were desirous of taking to themselves wives, and being too well-known as to honor in their own country, they took a journey into a far country and there procured for themselves wives."

Again, "Some also were casting dust and ashes toward heaven, and chief among them all was Josiah, blowing his bugle and making sound so great the neighboring hills and valleys echoed with the resounding acclamation."

This large-nosed Josiah was the same Josiah Crawford who required such stubborn payment for the borrowed book.

Later there was Aunt Rebecca's "Letter from the Lost Townships," Lincoln's most important contribution to political satir and perhaps the best indicator of the latent literary power that might have found its way in slighter and more entertaining rivulets if Lincoln's life had not been kept so rigorously in its proper, deep channel.

His natural taste was excellent. Was it a stubborn streak of rationalism or literary horror that caused him to refuse to sing the popular hymns, "How Tedious and Tasteless the Hours" and "Alas, and Did My Saviour Bleed?" True, he admired rather extravagantly "Why Should the Spirit of Mortal Be Proud?" because some chord in his nature was exactly attuned to the melancholy note struck by William Knox. But he knew there was better poetry, as his love of Burns, Shakespeare, Browning, and Whitman showed. The portrait painter, Carpenter, in his *Six Months in the White House*, tells how pertinently and how feelingly he would quote extended passages from Shakespeare, especially from *Macbeth, Hamlet,* and *Richard II.* The soliloquy of Claudius, "Oh, my offense is rank . . ." he thought finer than "To be or not to be." And he admired passionately that of Richard, "Now is the winter of our discontent." General Viele has recorded in *Harper's Monthly* how on a visit to Fortress Monroe Lincoln "would sit for hours during the trip, repeating the finest passages of Shakespeare's best plays, page after page of Browning [I cannot help thinking that a little bit of Browning went a long way with this good general] and whole cantos of Byron." Other poets known on sufficient evidence to have been favorites are Hood, Bryant, Whittier, Holmes, and Lowell. He knew Goldsmith well enough to hit off McClellan with a line from *The Deserted Village*, "Even his failings lean to virtue's side." Noah Brooks stated that Lincoln was a lover of many philosophical works, and cited Butler's *Analogy* and Mill on *Liberty*. An interesting foreign testimony is that of the Marquis de Chambroun: ". . . his judgment evinces that sort of delicacy and soundness of taste that would honor a great literary critic."

There are three overlapping periods in his life:

I. THE PHYSICAL PERIOD — YOUTH. Lincoln was not precocious; he grew up slowly and his delight in physical prowess lasted until his not very savory duel with Shields in 1842, when he was thirty-three.

II. THE PERIOD OF INTELLECTUAL EXPANSION. From the Black Hawk War, when, a captain at twenty-three, he assumed his first leadership over men, until 1860, when at fifty-one, in the Cooper Institute Speech, he reached his full intellectual maturity.

III. THE COMPLETE LINCOLN. From 1854, when he met Douglas on the Kansas-Nebraska Bill, and realized his moral and spiritual mastery. There was nothing of the holier-than-thou attitude in Lincoln's makeup; though he was a man without vices, he never bragged of his virtue. Nevertheless, Lincoln knew, as every strong man knows, wherein he was strong. No man was ever known to insult him with impunity. After 1854 Lincoln's character was fully integrated and there breathed from him a new dignity that not the patronage of Douglas, nor the open scorn of Stanton, nor the easy superiority of Seward, nor the arrogance of McClellan could taint. It was not merely that Lincoln was *patient* with these men; he had just translated his seventy-seven physical inches into a corresponding spiritual superiority. The keynote of Alonzo Rothschild's study, "Abraham Lincoln, Master of Men," is, "The spirit of mastery moved Abraham Lincoln at a very early age." My effort is to show that Lincoln gained mastery through the power of words, "words in the best order."

I. YOUTH

The first period, negligible from the point of view of final results, is all-important for foundations, and we should here note something of his technique. Lincoln's art of translating every situation into dramatic form created a new genre. His anecdotes and figures are (1) short, (2) dramatic, (3) kindly (almost always after his adolescent satires), (4) realistic,

180

(5) apt — always apt. Add to these (6) verbally felicitous, and all is said. Emerson wrote shortly after the assassination, "If Lincoln had lived in primitive times, his fables would have made him fabulous." Have they not indeed made him fabulous?

Nothing will take the place of a dip into Sandburg's great magazine of anecdotes. My two favorites from the early years are related to his short congressional experience. The first everyone remembers: when Peter Cartwright, Lincoln's formidable clerical opponent, demanded in a revival service that all who wanted to go to heaven should rise, he asked Lincoln who had remained seated, "Mr. Lincoln, where do you want to go?" "Oh," said Lincoln, unlimbering and rising to his full height, "I'm going to Congress." The other was as devastating to his opponent, a representative from Michigan who had presidential aspirations. This was the story of the farmer who, standing on his porch, took three shots at what he thought was a squirrel in a nearby tree. The old man's son, aghast at his father's poor marksmanship, and seeing no squirrel in the tree, came up, stared into his father's face, then, greatly relieved, guffawed, "Dad, you're shootin' at a louse on your eyelash."

It is not irrelevant here to glance at his picturesque language in official years, which shows the constant play of imagination. When a policy was demanded of him, he said he had none; he was just "living in a tent during a storm and driving in pegs as fast as they were blown out." "A presidential chin-fly" made Stanton's department go. Sending troops to McClellan was like "shovelling fleas across a barn floor: so many got lost on the way." In a telegram to Hooker he wrote, "If the head of Lee's army is at Martinsburg and the tail of it on the plank road between Fredericksburg and Chancellorsville the animal must be slim somewhere, could you not break him?"

The letter to Colonel Robert Allen relative to an insinuation of a dark secret that Allen could reveal if he would is

181

an illustration of refined irony that speaks well for the four years of self-discipline since his first political speech.

"No one has needed favors more than I, and generally, few have been less unwilling to accept them; but in this case favor to me would be injustice to the public, and therefore I must beg your pardon for declining it. That I once had the confidence of the people of Sangamon is sufficiently evident; and if I have since done anything, either by design or misadventure, which, if known would subject me to a forfeiture of that confidence, he that knows of the thing and conceals it is a traitor to his country's interest. . . . I am flattered with the personal regard you manifested for me; but I do hope that upon mature reflection, you will view the public interest as a paramount consideration, and therefore determine to let the worst come. I here assure you that the candid statement of facts on your part, however low it may sink me, shall never break the tie of personal friendship between us. I wish an answer to this, and you are at liberty to publish both if you choose.

Very respectfully,
A. LINCOLN.

This is sheer perfection — for its purpose. The literary qualities are sufficiently manifest to the ear, but one needs to scrutinize the detailed structure to appreciate how far Lincoln had come in four years of grinding discipline.

II. EXPANSION

The second period must be passed over quickly. Of some men's success it could be said, "He had a friend." Of Lincoln's it can be said: "He had many friends, because he was friend to many; but more important, he had an opponent to measure himself by." Stephen A. Douglas was a man of fine natural ability and immense personal magnetism. But unlike Lincoln he had no passion for the truth of the spoken word and had not learned the art of appeal through the written word. Despite his earlier and much more propitious entry into public place, from the time when he and Lincoln used to argue around the stove in Josh Speed's Springfield store, when both were members of the legislature, it was a foregone conclusion that the ultimate victory would rest with the long, sprawling, humorous, self-contained airedale of a man who used words so scrupulously; not with the short, compact, dogmatic, pugnacious bulldog of a man who threw words around with scant respect. Douglas was Lincoln's anvil on which he hammered out the first rude models of his political philosophy; had he been a softer anvil, Lincoln's steel would not have been so evenly and finely tempered.

I shall confine myself to a notice of but seven compositions of this period.

The first is a letter written to Mrs. O. H. Browning in 1838, giving the history of his second love romance, very unromantic, with Mary Owen. Only a complete reading will give an adequate sense of the sprightliness and flexibility that Lincoln's pen had learned.

After reading this and the letter to Robert Allen, so notable in restraint, it will be all the more shocking to consider that famous sentence in a letter to his comrade, Speed, in 1841, while his engagement to Mary Todd was still hanging in the balance, "If what I feel were distributed to the whole human family, there would not be one cheerful face on earth." It is irrelevant to enter here into a discussion of his love affairs, but no one can deny the startling power of that hyperbole. Had Lincoln not been so isolated, so reticent, and had tried to express what was in his heart, we might have had a scrap of psychological analysis far surpassing in interest the letter to Mrs. Browning.

The peroration to a temperance address the next year

contains the last bit of fustian to be found in his writings. It marks the end of his tendency to verse rhythms. It was on Washington's birthday anniversary: "To add brightness to the sun or glory to the name of Washington is alike impossible. Let none attempt it. In solemn awe pronounce the name, and in its naked, deathless splendor leave it shining on." Not without effect after all, but not the harmonies of the Second Inaugural. It is not without significance that in a lecture on "Discoveries and Inventions" during this period he marvels most at the invention of language.

The next four compositions I must dismiss with a bare mention:

Notes for a law lecture, July 1851.

A speech at Peoria, October 16, 1854, on the repeal of the Missouri Compromise.

The so-called Lost Speech at Bloomington, at the official organization of the Republican party in 1856. (A critical analysis of the resuscitated text of this speech published by *McClure's* and since in various collections, has led Angle and other students to conclude that the speech is still "lost.")

The seven debates with Douglas in 1858. A notable literary feature is the allegory about the conspiracy involving Franklin (Pierce), Roger (Taney), James (Buchanan), and Stephen (Douglas).

Finally, and climactically, the Cooper Institute Speech, 1860. Stephenson calls this "the best fortified as well as the most convincing and effective political address of an argumentative nature before an American audience up to that time." Even cantankerous old Horace Greeley said, "the best political address to which I ever listened — and I have heard some of Webster's grandest." Lincoln took as text a statement of Douglas': "Our Fathers, when they framed the government under which we live, understood this question just as well, and even better, than we do now." No candidate for the doctorate ever proceeded by a sounder method of research; no orator ever mingled better just the right proportion of dignity and familiarity. He made good use of his fundamental technique of allegory. "But you," speaking to the South, "will not abide the election of a Republican President! In that supposed event, you say, you will destroy the Union; and then, you say, the great crime of having destroyed it will be upon us! That is cool. A highwayman holds a pistol to my ear, and mutters through his teeth, 'Stand and deliver or I shall kill you, and then you will be a murderer.'"

This address was the climax of his years of preparation. Hardly a line after this but shows the stamp of the complete man of letters.

III. THE FINAL PERIOD

The exhibits here could be many. One of the most interesting involves a close scrutiny of detail, and perhaps it will be found rewarding to give it the requisite time and space. The final paragraph of the First Inaugural was in substance a suggestion by Secretary of State Seward.

Seward's suggestion: "I close. We are not, we must not be, aliens or enemies, but fellow-countrymen and brethren. Although passion has strained our bonds of affection too hardly, they must not, I am sure they will not, be broken. The mystic chords which, proceeding from so many battlefields and so many patriot graves, pass through all the hearts and all hearths in this broad continent of ours, will yet again harmonize in their ancient music when breathed upon by the guardian angel of the nation."*

Lincoln's final paragraph: "I am loath to close. We are not enemies, but friends. We must not be enemies. Though passion may have strained, it must not break our bonds of affection. The mystic chords of memory, stretching from every battlefield and patriot grave to every living heart and hearthstone all over this broad land will yet swell the chorus

*From Nicolay and Hay, *Abraham Lincoln: a History*, Vol. III.

of the Union when again touched, as surely they will be, by the better angels of our nature."

Now a patient comparison:

"I am loath to close." The paragraph is shortened from 84 words to 75, yet this sentence contains five words instead of Seward's two. The gain is in the rhythm, which carries the tone of conciliation that Lincoln is aiming at.

"We are not enemies, but friends." Seward was not quite sure that "we are not aliens or enemies." He reconsiders in the same sentence, "we must not be aliens or enemies." This shows the unsure phrase for exactly what it was, wishful thinking, with faint hope. Lincoln voices a clear directive for the present, and a directive hope for the future.

". . . it must not break our bonds of affection." Again Lincoln avoids the anticlimactic tone of the original and states a simple, hortatory hope.

"The mystic chords" said Seward; but what mystic chords he did not know. ". . . of memory," added Lincoln, reaching into Seward's high level of abstraction and attaching the chords to a node, giving them a referent, "memory."

Was it his study of Newman's *Practical System of Rhetoric* or a natural instinct that caused Lincoln to reject the loose plurals in "battlefields and patriot graves" for the tight, specific "every battlefield and patriot grave"? Whatever his reason, the change was effective.

". . . this broad land" has nothing of the grandiosity and the patronizing possessiveness of "this broad continent of ours."

Instead of vague "ancient music" Lincoln hears "the chorus of the Union." And the frigid and meaningless "guardian angel of the nation" becomes in Lincoln's warm imagination "the better angels of our nature," creatures in which he could believe.

Lincoln recognized the essential and basic propriety in Seward's suggestion of the value of concluding with an emotional appeal; and accepted a generous gift in a generous spirit. He did what successful literary borrowers have always done, recreated in imagination the framework of the accepted idea and clothed it in fresh and meaningful imagery. Happy ghost-writer Seward, who could furnish a president the warp for such a woof as Lincoln wove!

A letter from Secretary Seward to C. F. Adams, Minister to Great Britain. In G. F. Baker's *Forms of Public Discourse* is reprinted Seward's original draft, with Lincoln's interpolations and emendations, which were incorporated in the final dispatch. Had Seward's belligerent note been sent, war with Great Britain might have resulted in 1861.

The Open Letter to Horace Greeley, August 22, 1862, is widely known. It shows perfectly the patient, cautious but firm Lincoln symbolized by Herndon's description of the way he walked, lifting his foot and putting it down as a whole foot, not heel and toe, bending the knees a little, and consequently never slipping. If anyone ever failed to get what Lincoln meant him to get out of that letter, he has never revealed himself; he certainly could not pass the GI English test.

An open letter to the working men of Manchester, January 19, 1863.

Open letter to James C. Conkling, August 26, 1863. This is the letter that Lincoln himself thought "pretty good." It contained at least one line of great spontaneous poetry: "The Father of Waters again goes unvexed to the sea."

The Letter to Mrs. Bixby has been the center of some inconsequential squabbling, in no way touching its merit. The reader must agree up to a point with Stuart Sherman: "One can hardly read the letter through with dry eyes; and yet reading it makes one very happy. It makes one happy because it renders one in imagination a sharer of that splendid sacrifice, that solemn pride, that divine consolation. It makes one happy because it uplifts the heart and purges it of private interests, and admits one into the higher and more spacious, and grander life of the nation . . . It is the work of a great artist. Was it Lincoln? Or was it the America of our dreams?"

I do not subscribe to Sherman's theory that it was one of his Platonic absolutes that willy-nilly took the pen and wrote. It was Lincoln who guided the pen, the pen of the Indiana-Illinois rail-splitter.

The Gettysburg Memorial, November 19, 1863. This is a poem. I do not call it a poem because it has been thrown into blank verse — rather imperfect blank verse, for it is great prose — but because it is, by Coleridge's inspired definition, "the best words in the best order." It is a poem because it was designed, subconsciously I think, not to be heard by a few thousand people on that dreary November day in 1863, but to be *over*-heard by myriads through the ages. In 1913, Earl Curzon, Chancellor of the University of Oxford, addressing an assembly at Cambridge on the subject, "Modern British Eloquences," said in his conclusion that there are three supreme masterpieces of eloquence: the Funeral Oration of Pericles, and two of Lincoln's speeches, the Gettysburg Address and the Second Inaugural. "I escape," said he, "the task of deciding which is the masterpiece of modern English eloquence by awarding the prize to an American."

The Second Inaugural, March 4, 1865. Another poem! There was no need, as there had been four years before, of argument. Also there must not sound a paean of victory. What we have is a poem, a solemn hymn of praise and a solemn dedication to the greater tasks of peace. Its concluding strains will be heard by other centuries and other peoples who pay no heed to Bryant and Longfellow, perhaps not even to Poe and Whitman. The perfection of its mood and its music will charm unborn generations who will

188

scarcely be conscious that the American Civil War was once an all-important present.

There is no anticlimax in the Last Public Address on April 11, four days before his assassination. There is the same sustained power applied to practical uses, the calm, sure voice of Father Abraham, saying that he is planning for the future.

It might not be unprofitable to set down a list of recognized world classics in various types of literary expression and opposite them a list of the best America has to offer to discover whether in our short national life we have produced works worthy of that distinguished company. After inspection we should hesitate to claim a poet, novelist, or dramatist who deserves a seat among the half-dozen most eminent poets, novelists, and dramatists. But might we not dare to believe that in the long avenue of time the humorous fables of Abraham Lincoln and the Gettysburg Ode and the Second Inaugural will be enrolled as the contributions of America to the masterpieces of the world?

America to the World

My country heaps the dower of the world
With two gifts unshamed beside the Hebrew's song,
Deep Lao-tze's wisdom, and the tales that throng
The isles of Greece; the gems impearled
In Louvre and Vatican, the flag unfurled
From Shakespeare's tower, or those words winged along
The trackless chaos, avenues of wrong
Where fallen Lucifer his curses hurled.

"With malice toward none, with charity for all"—
Breathes forth the one, with open, outstretched hands.
"The sweetest, wisest soul of all my days and lands,"
The other, whispering to the future, thrall
Of him he loved. "You look like a man," said Lincoln,
While America says, "These both are men."